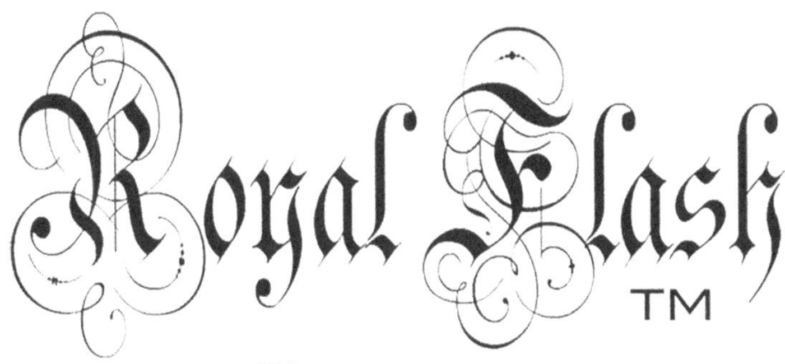

Presents

"
Flowers,Snakes,Birds,Owls & Koi
Coloring Book
"

All Artwork by

Cort Bengtson

Published by

Cort's Royal Ink Tattoo Company

Book Design and Layout by Cort Bengtson

Copyright 2017

All images are on file with

The Library of Congress

 ISBN-13: 978-1-948187-09-1

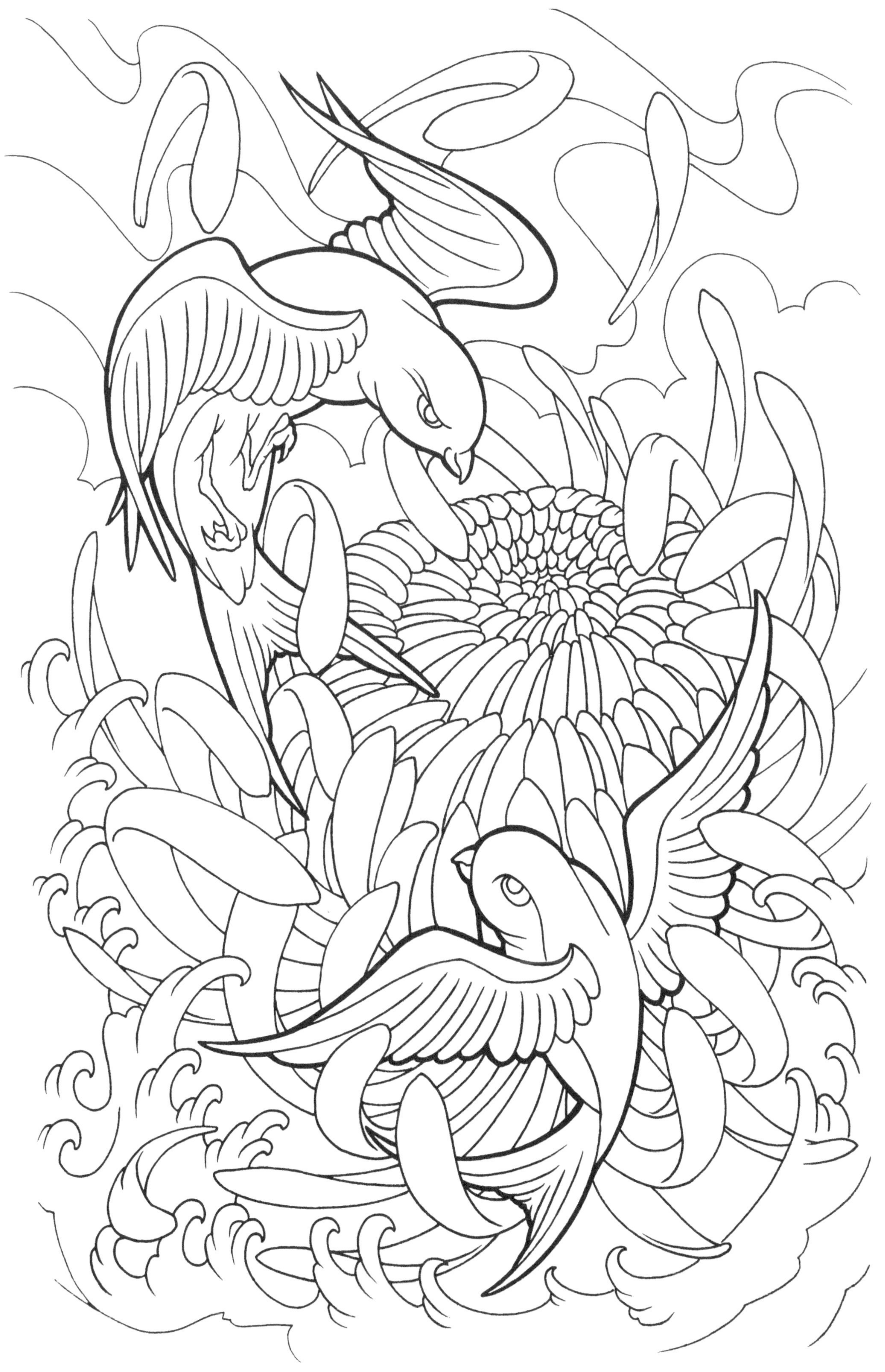

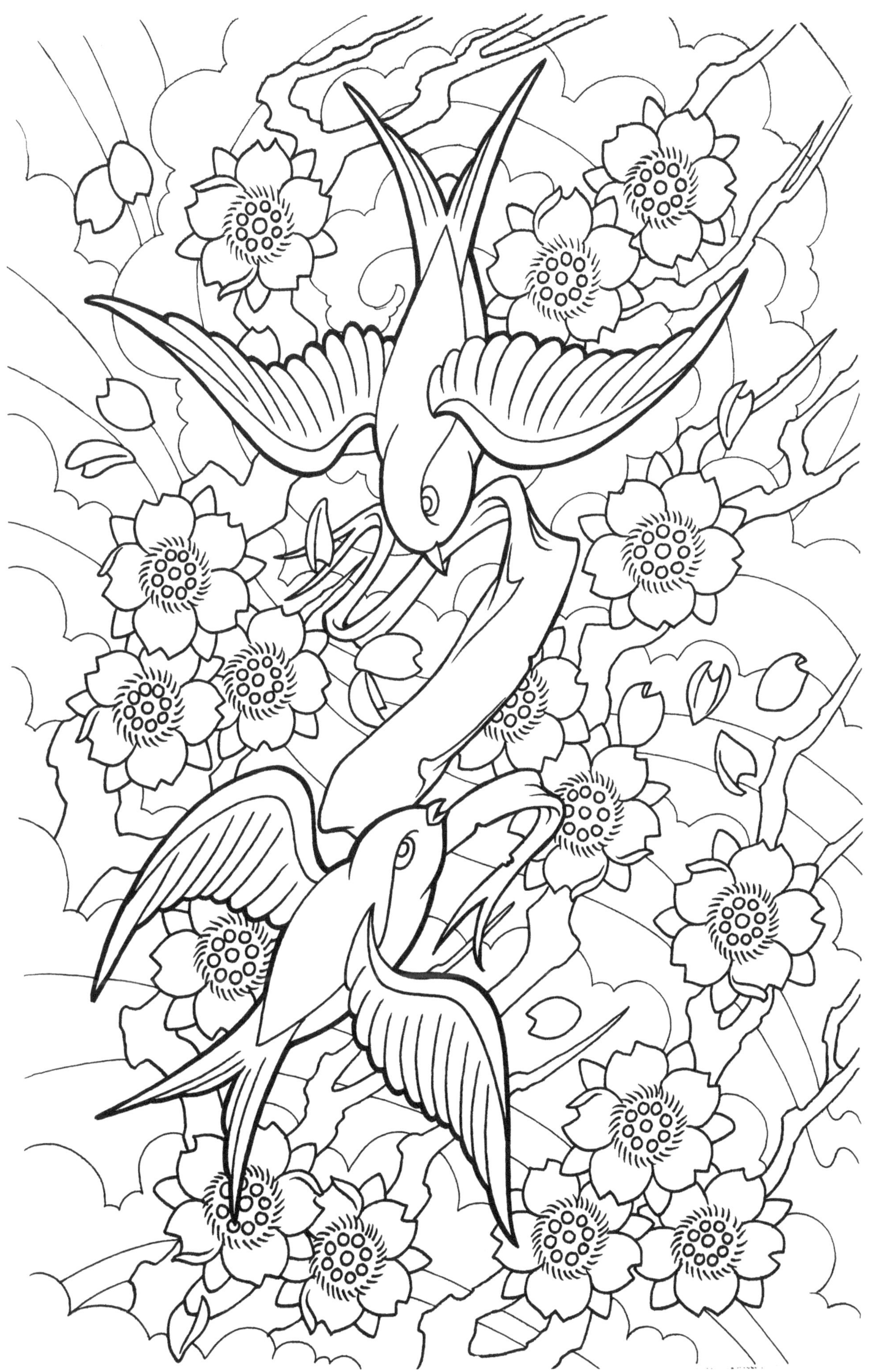

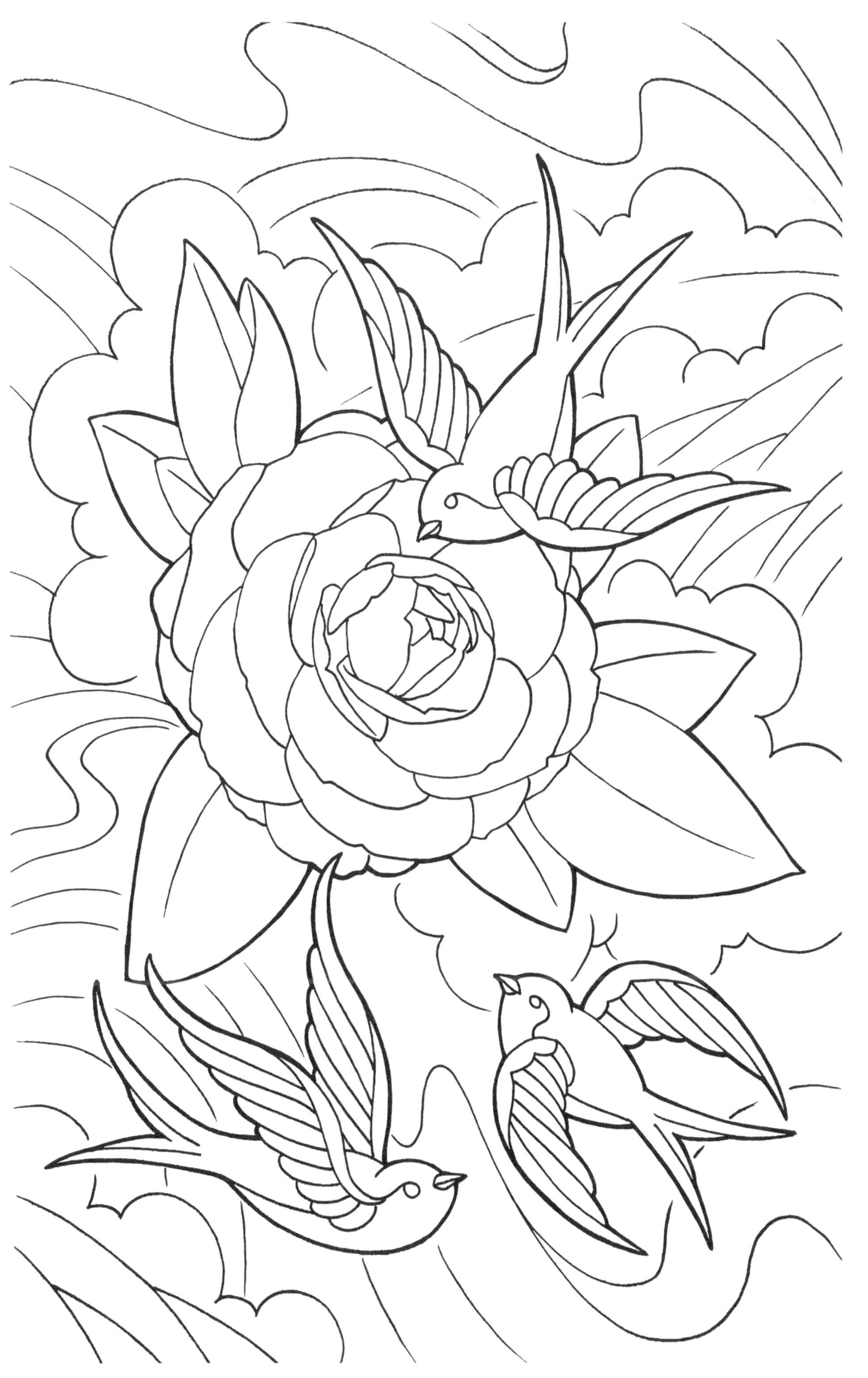

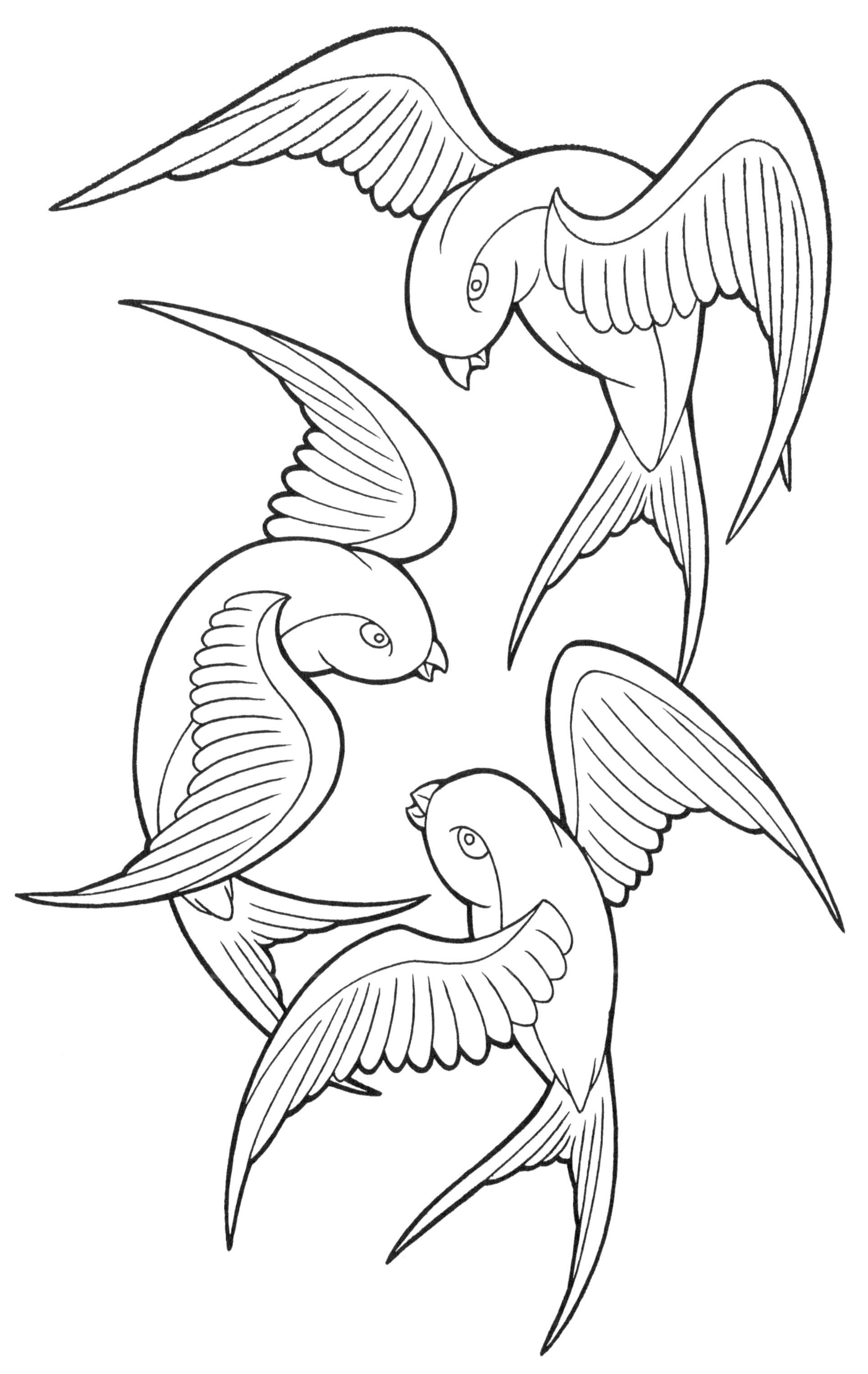

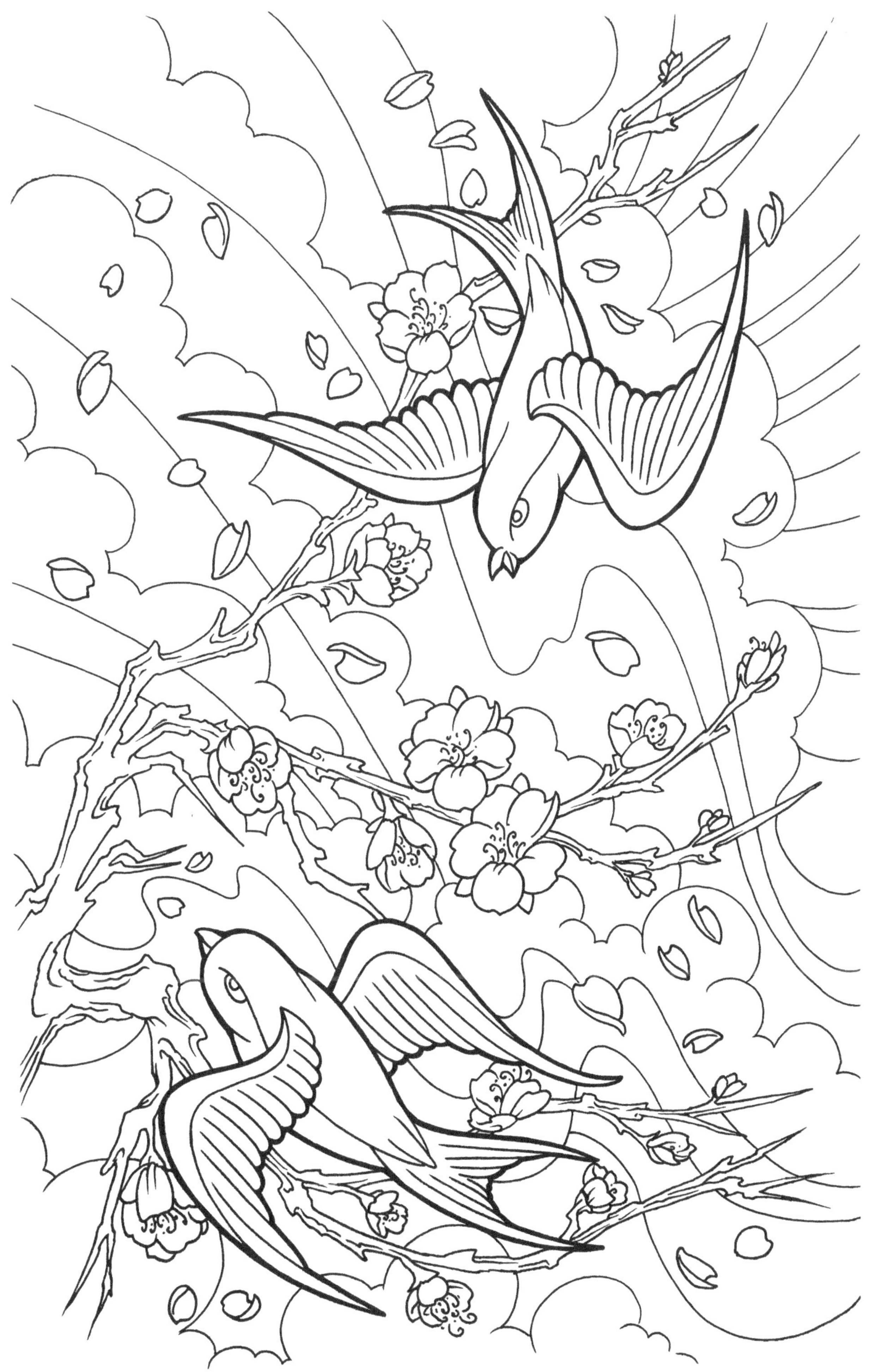

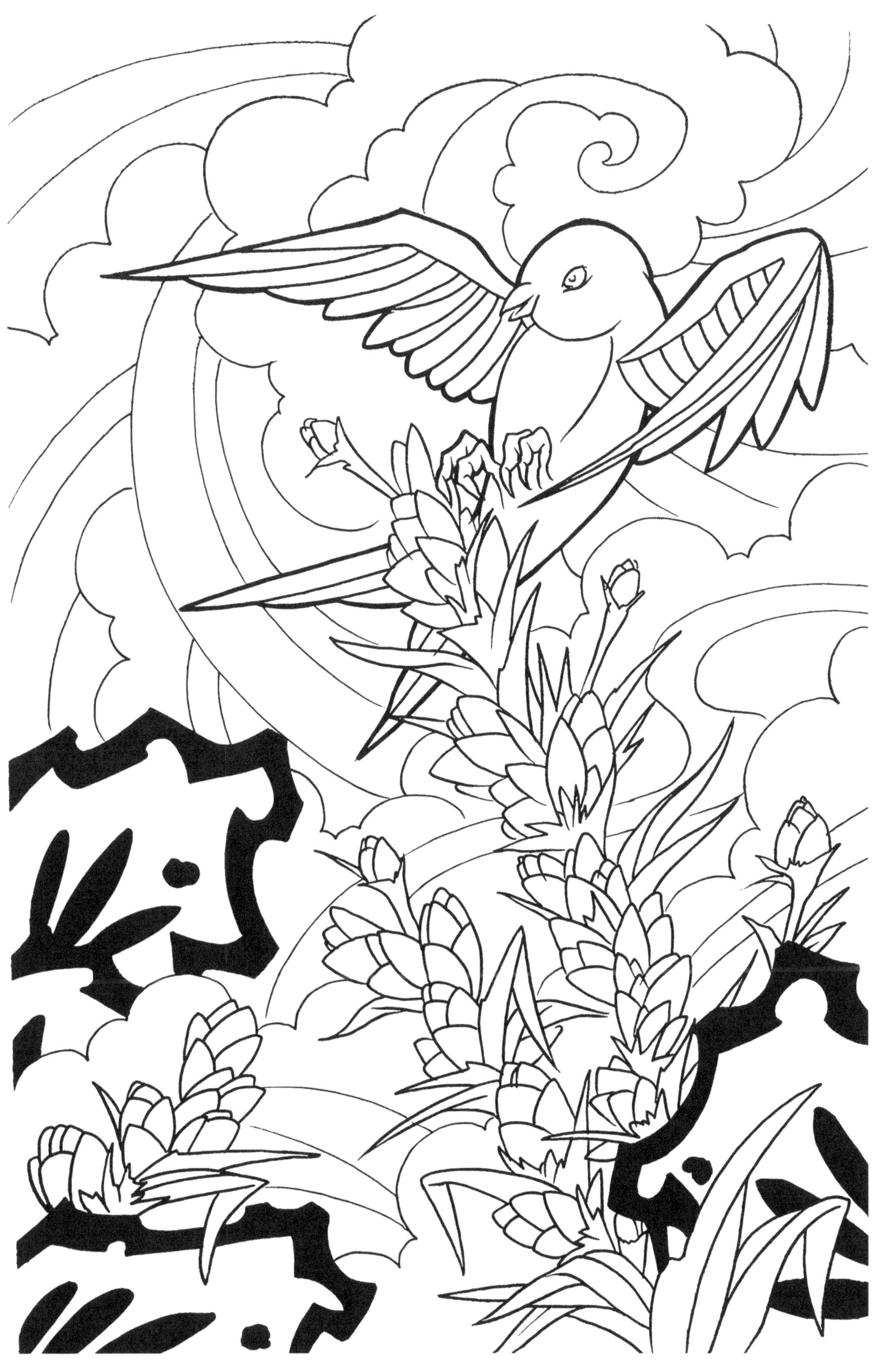

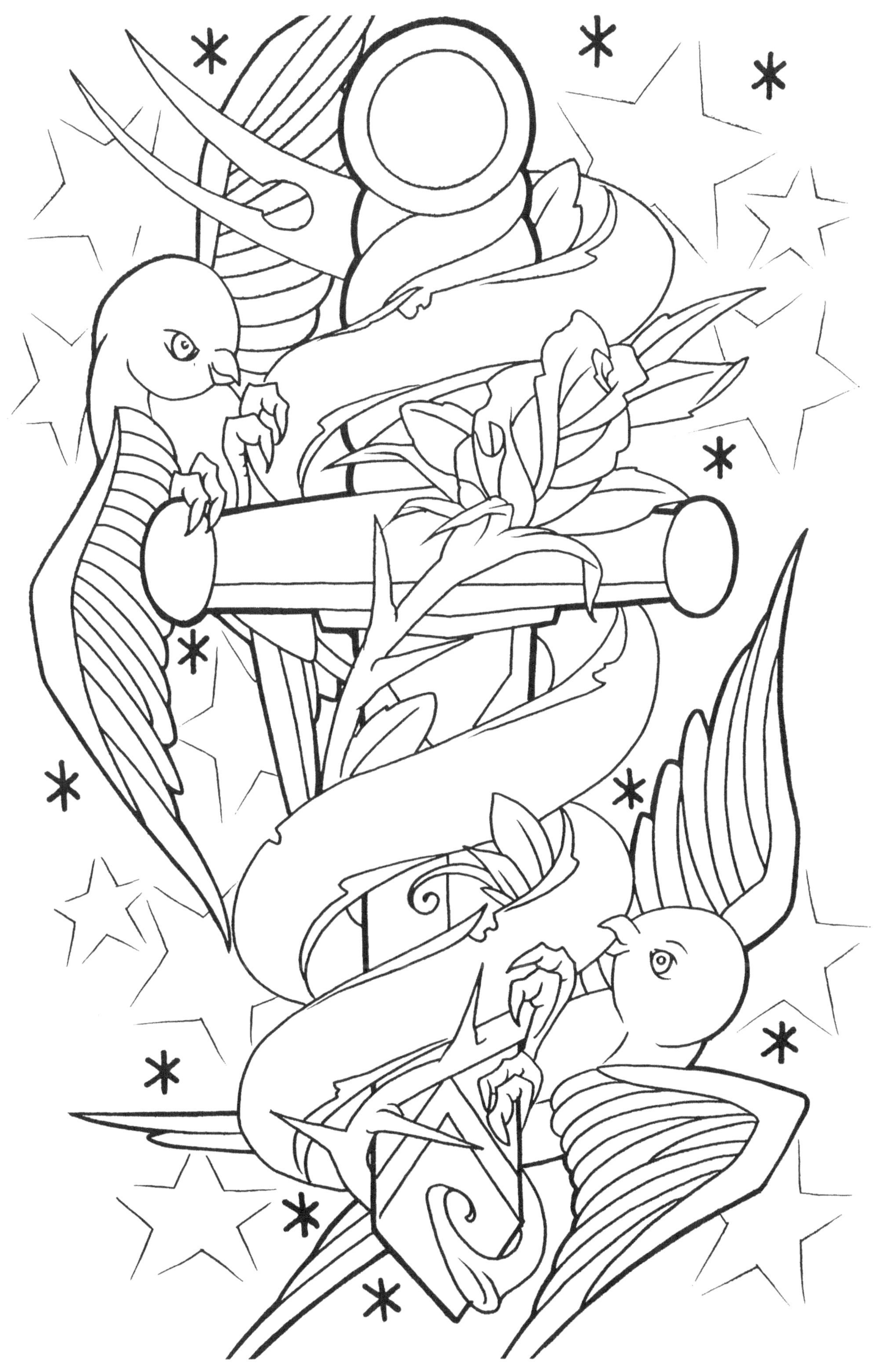

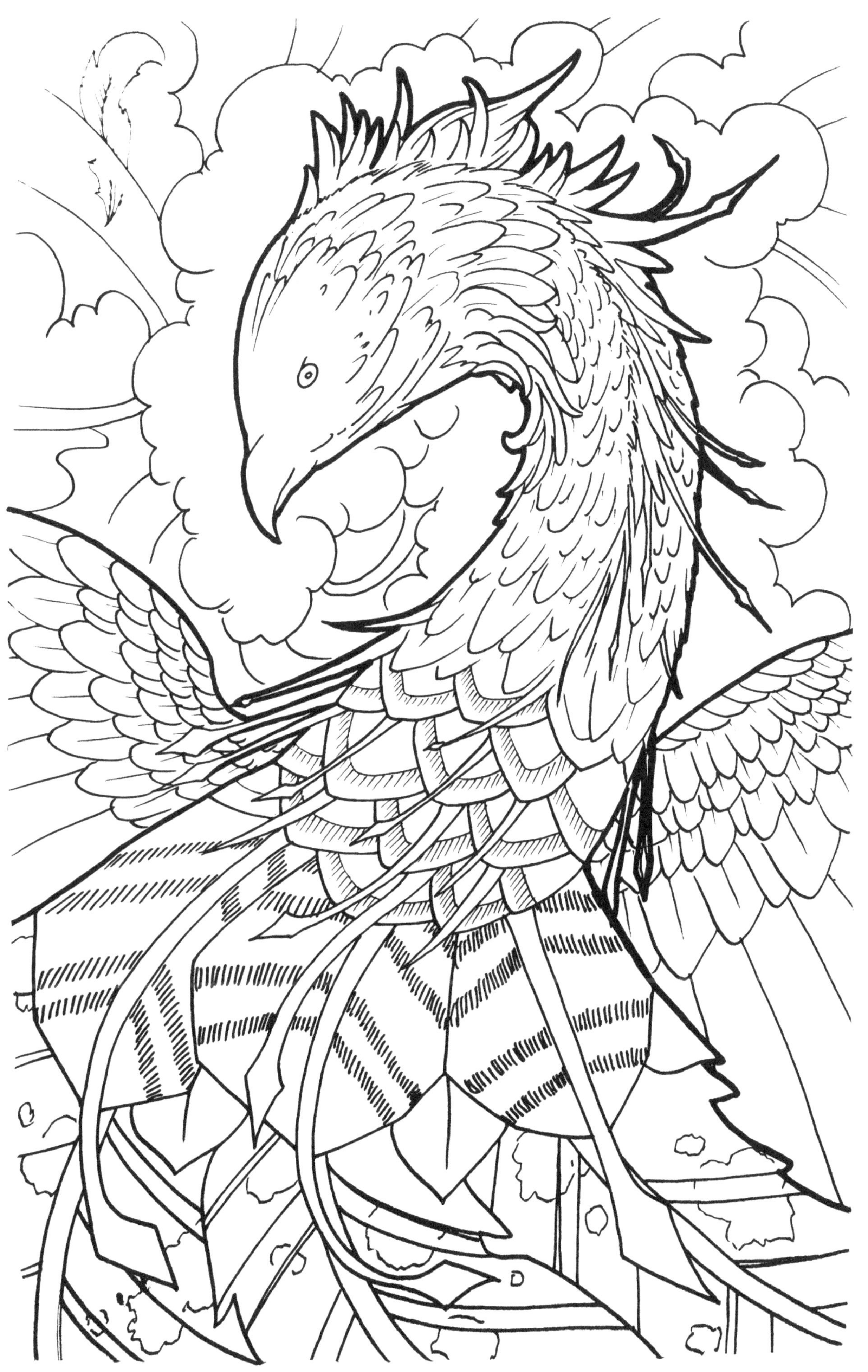

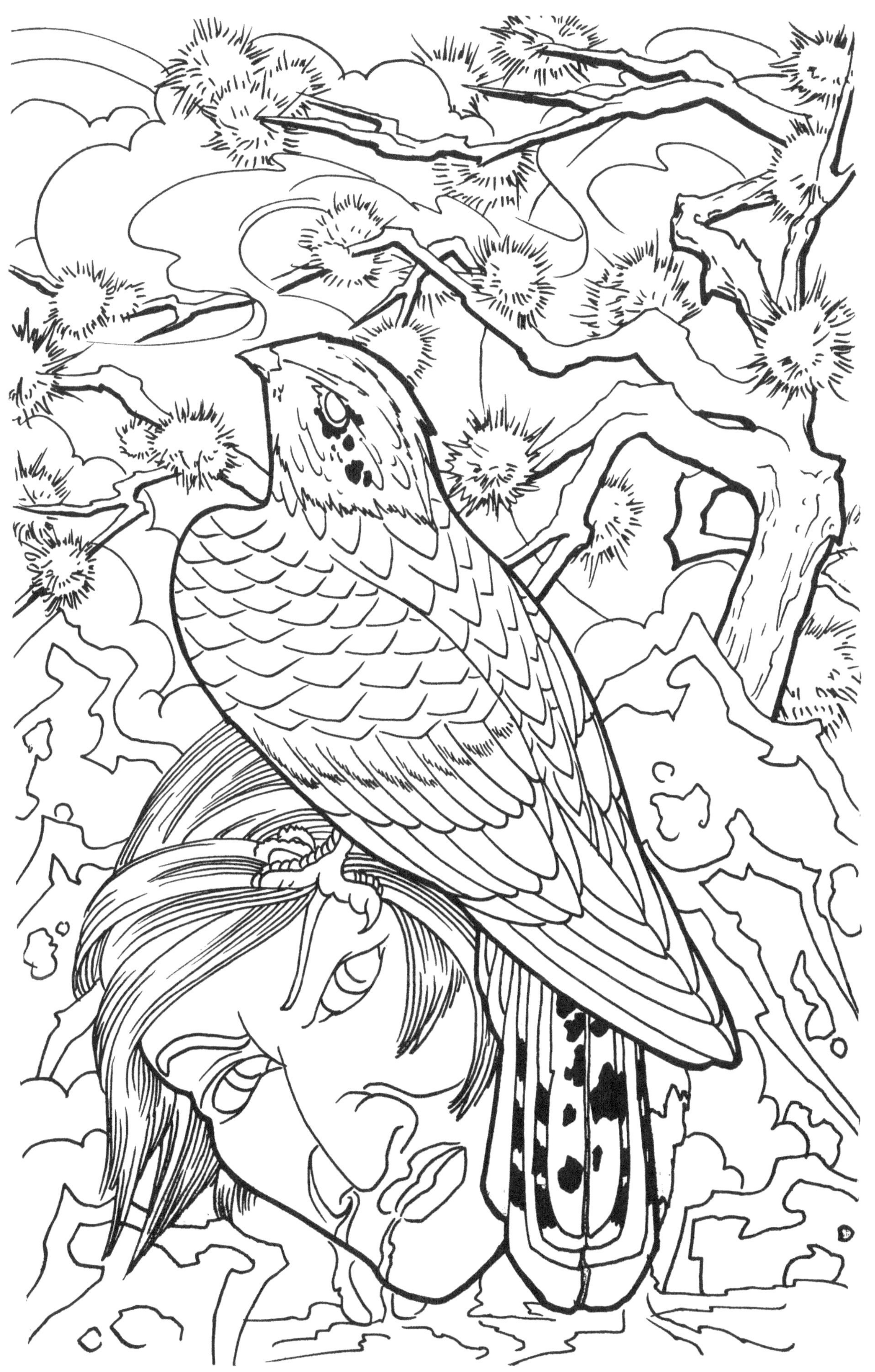

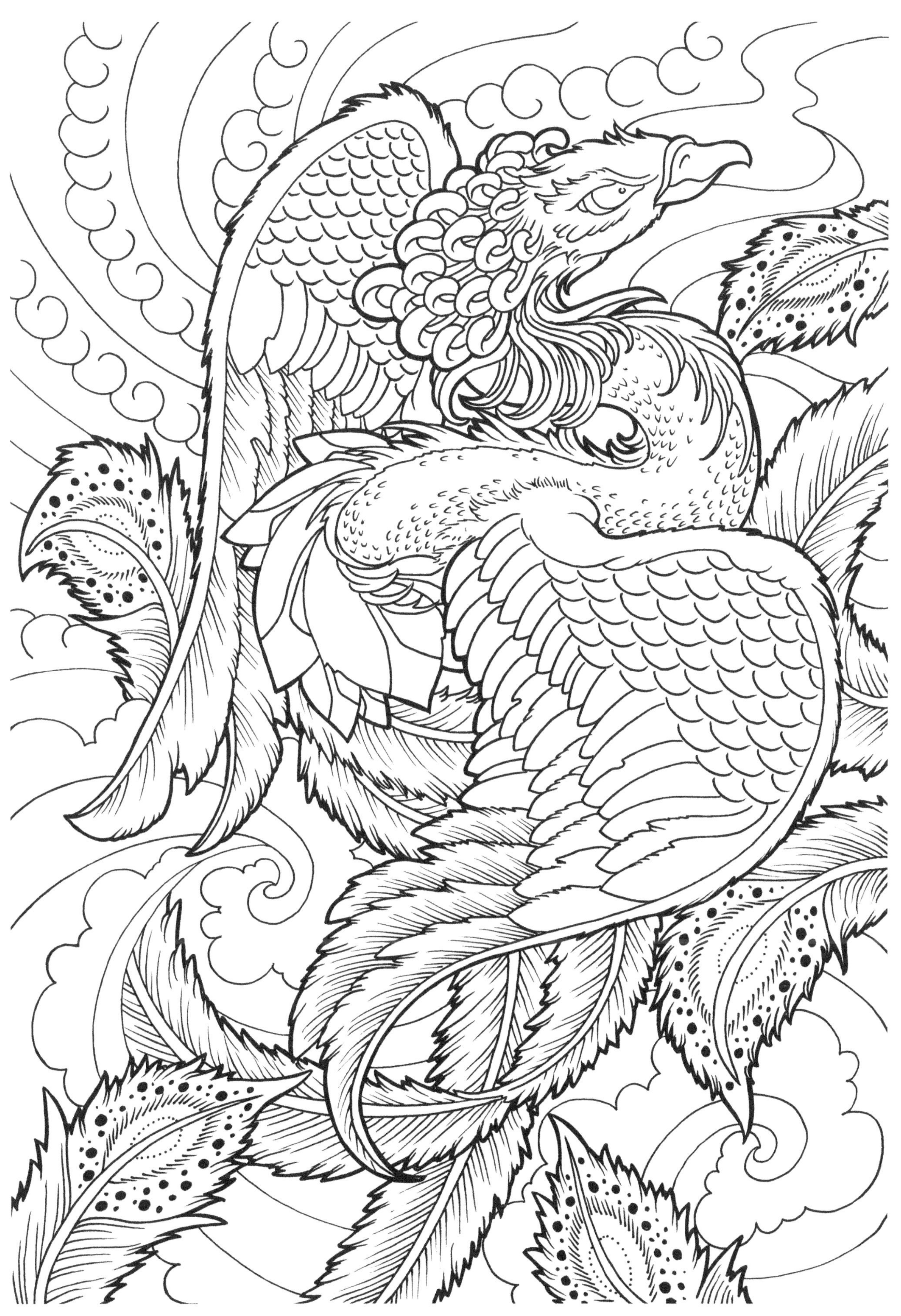

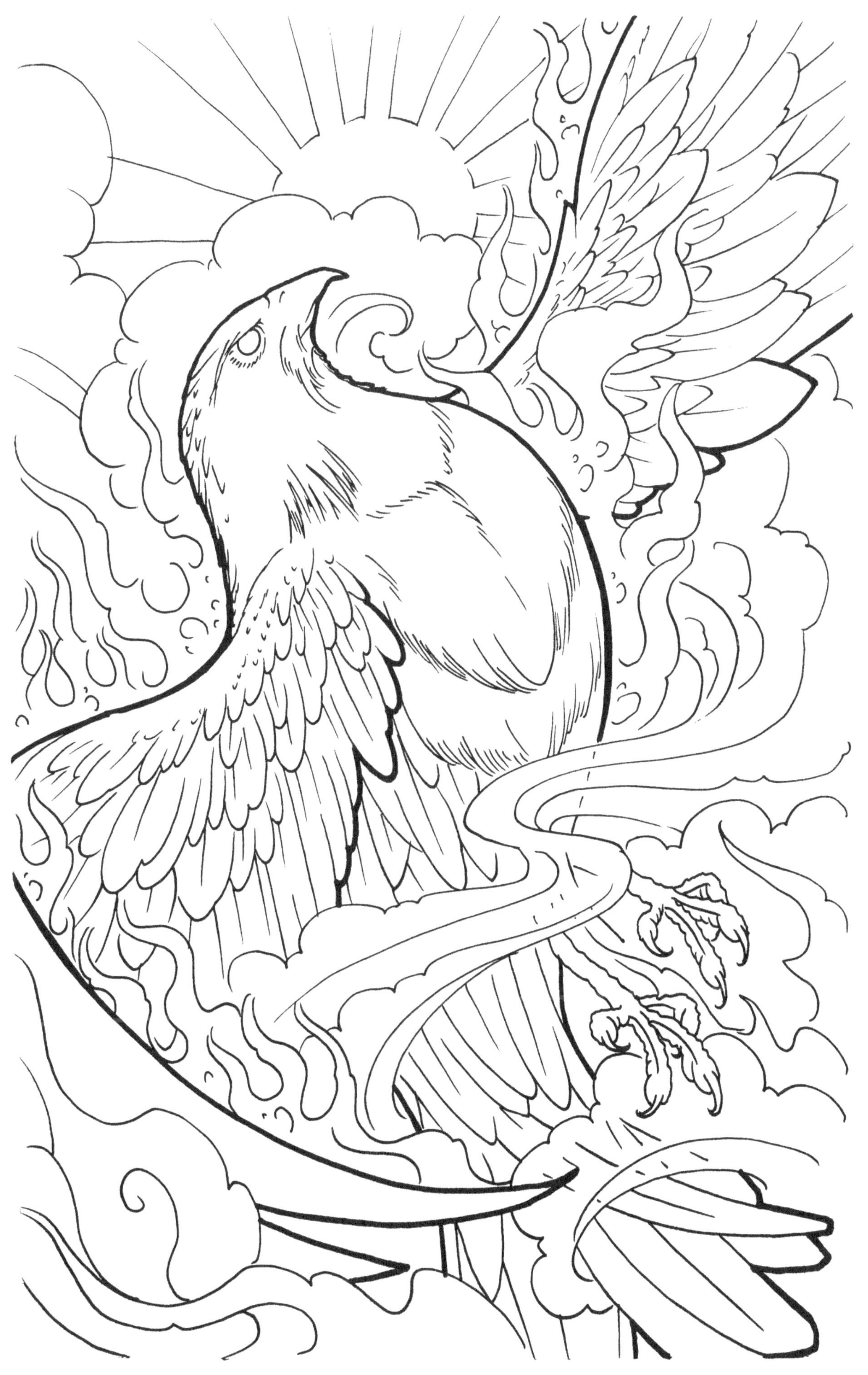

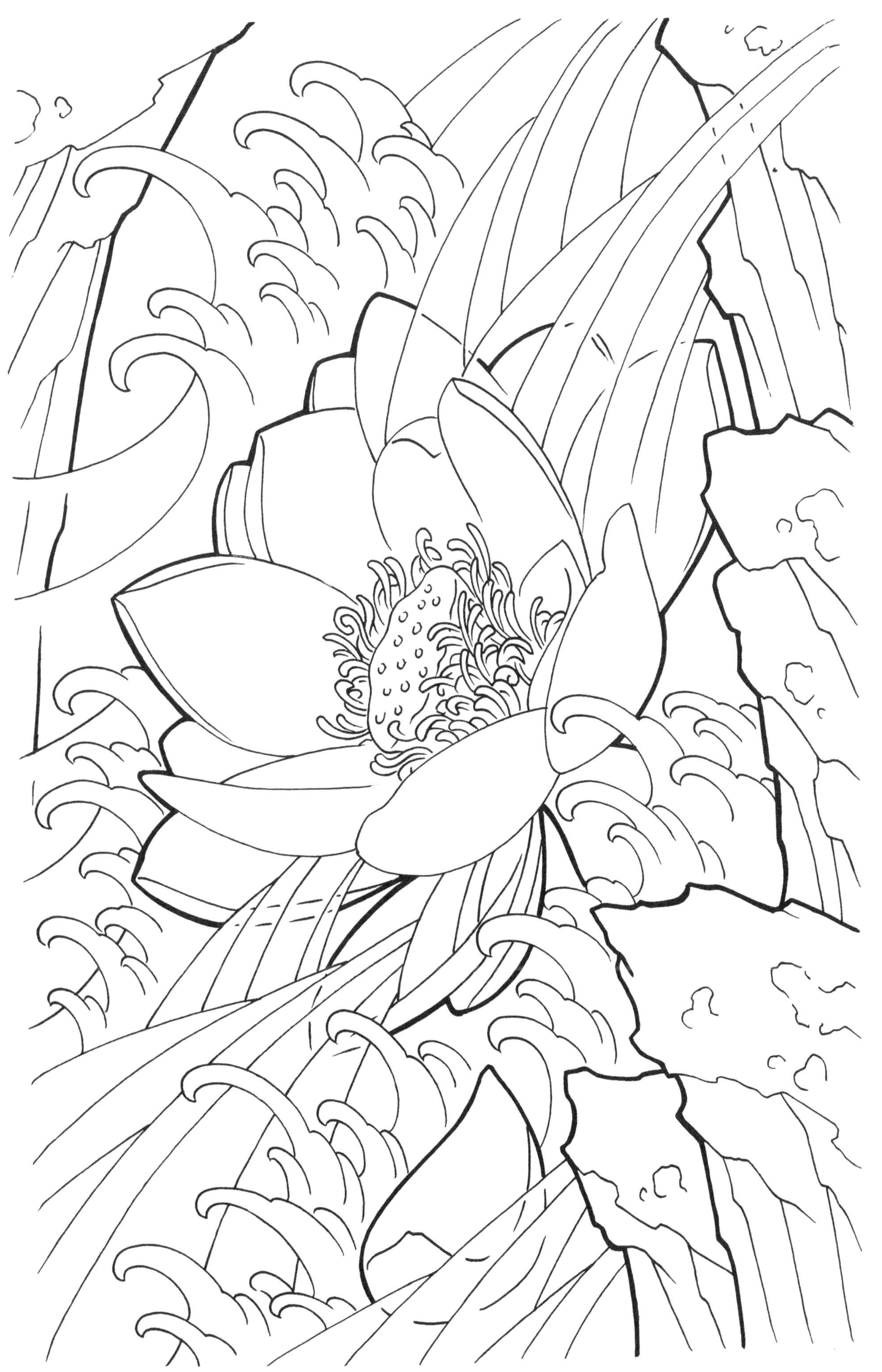

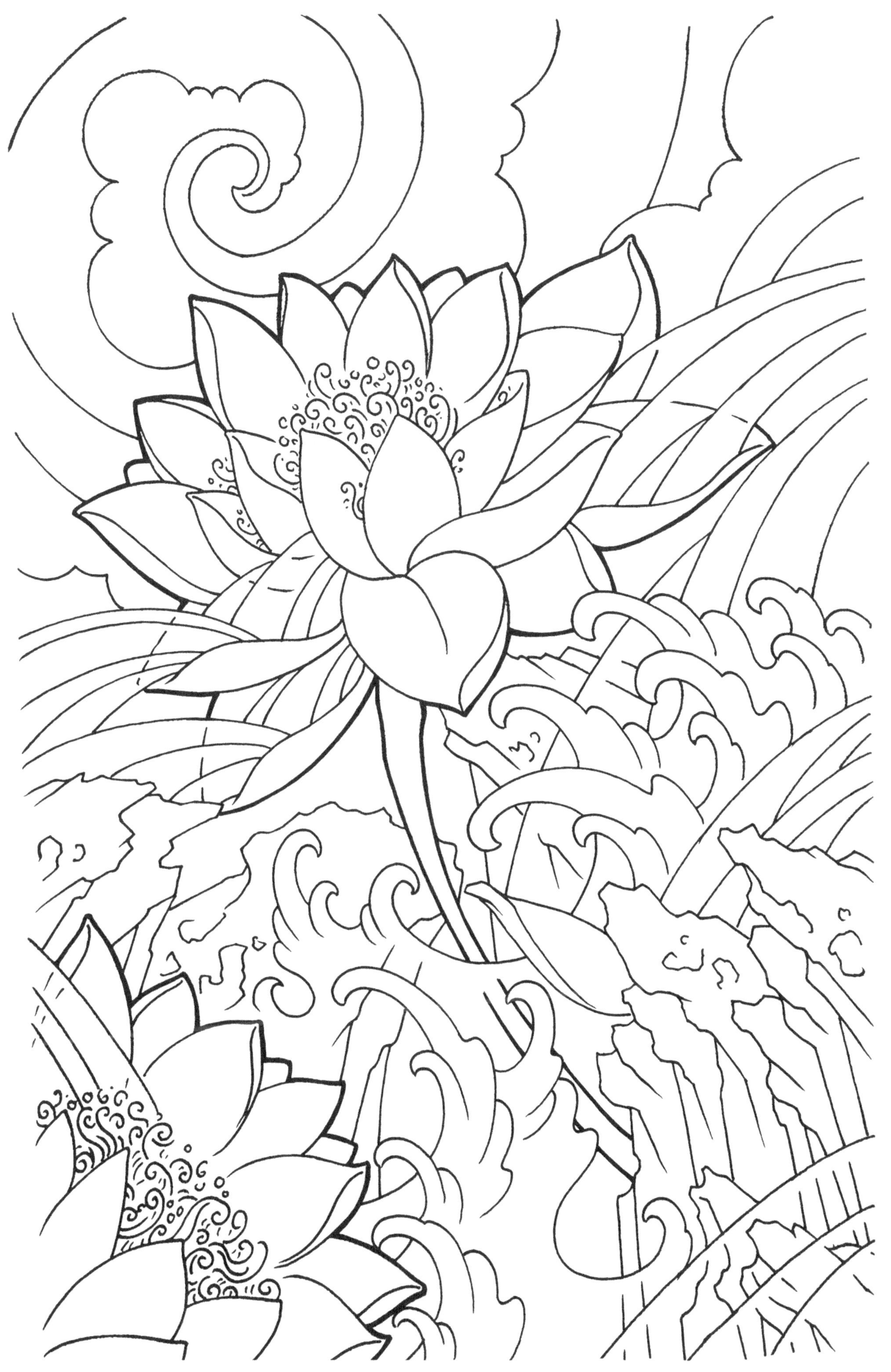

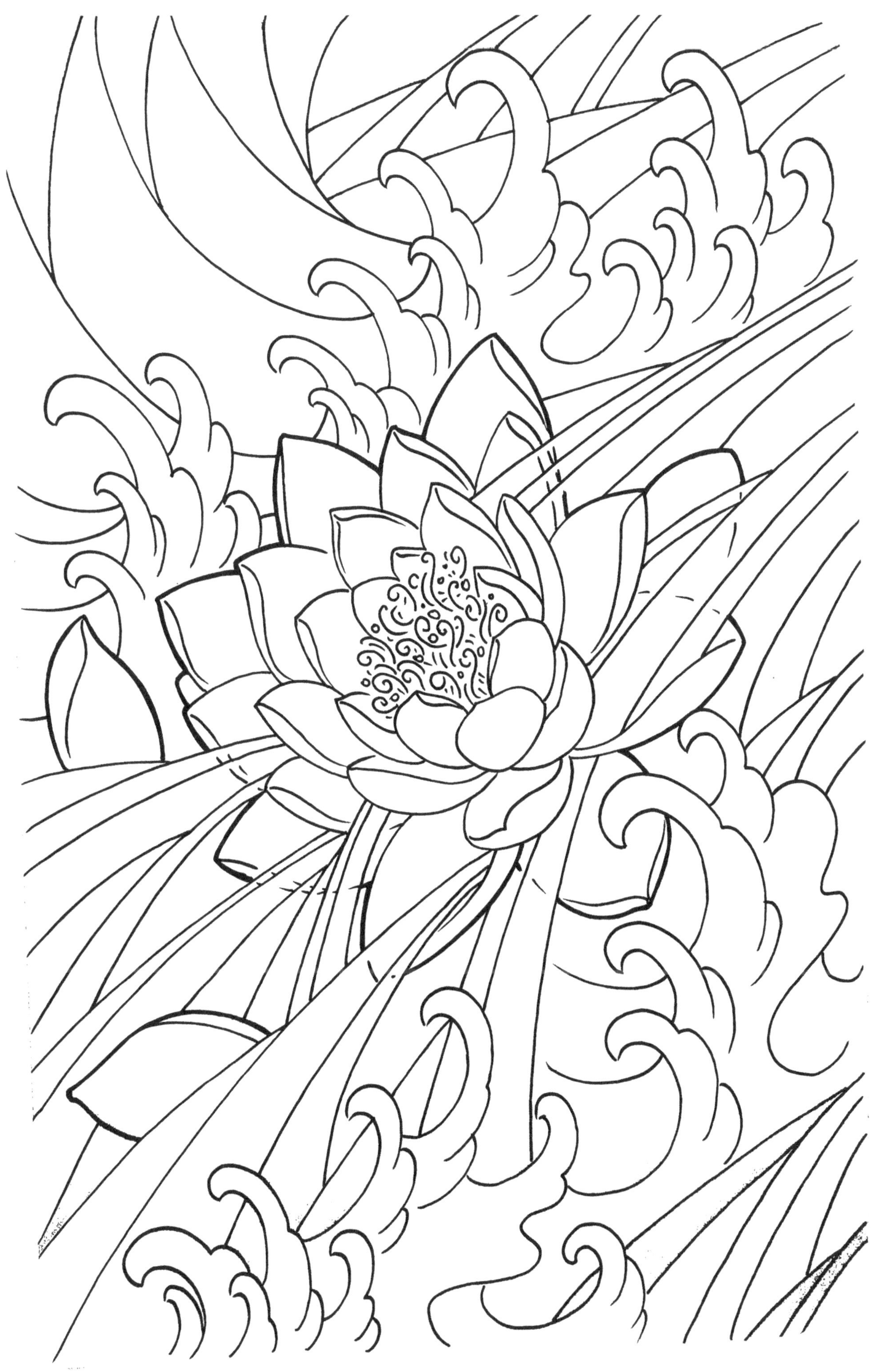

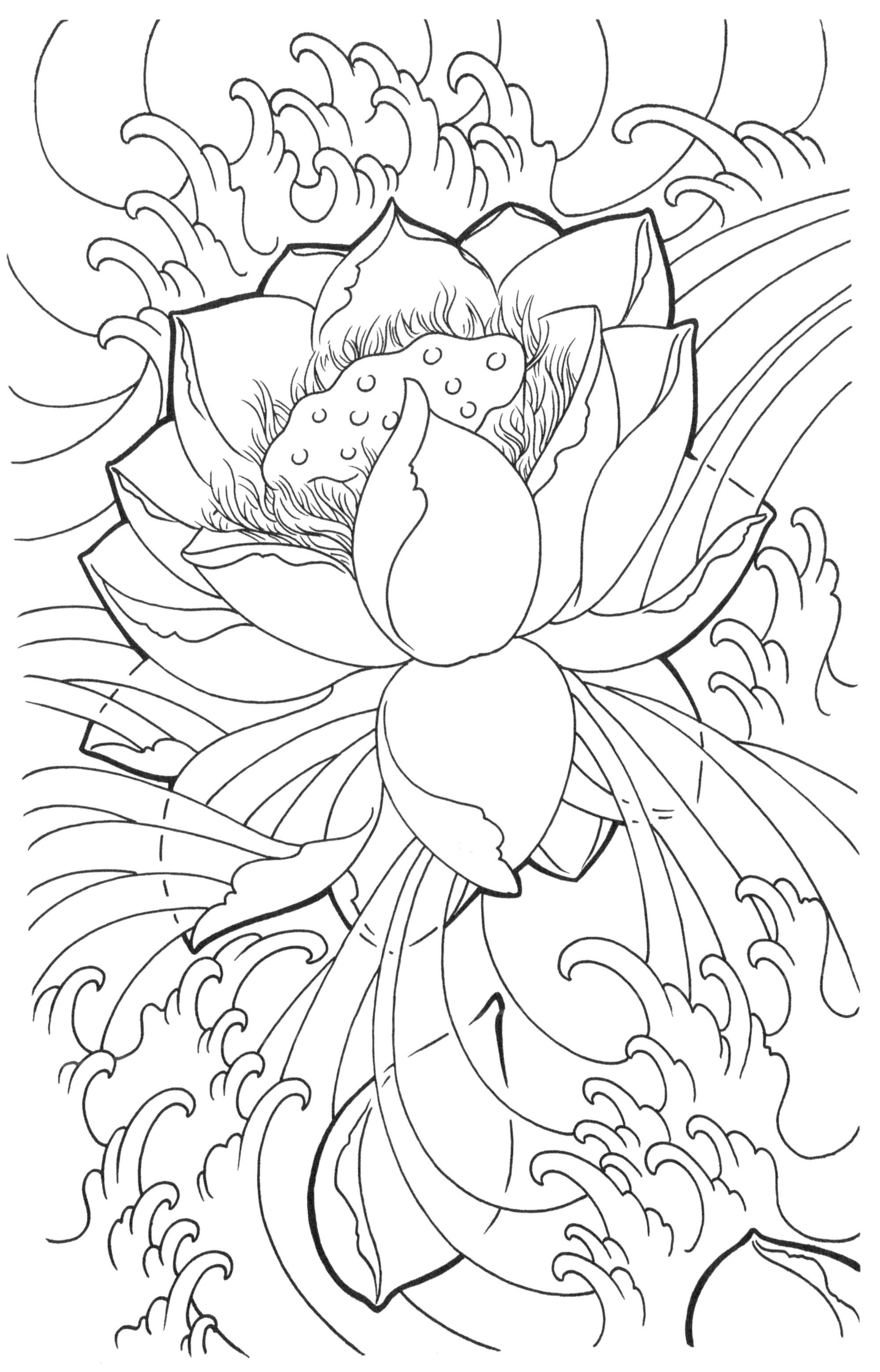

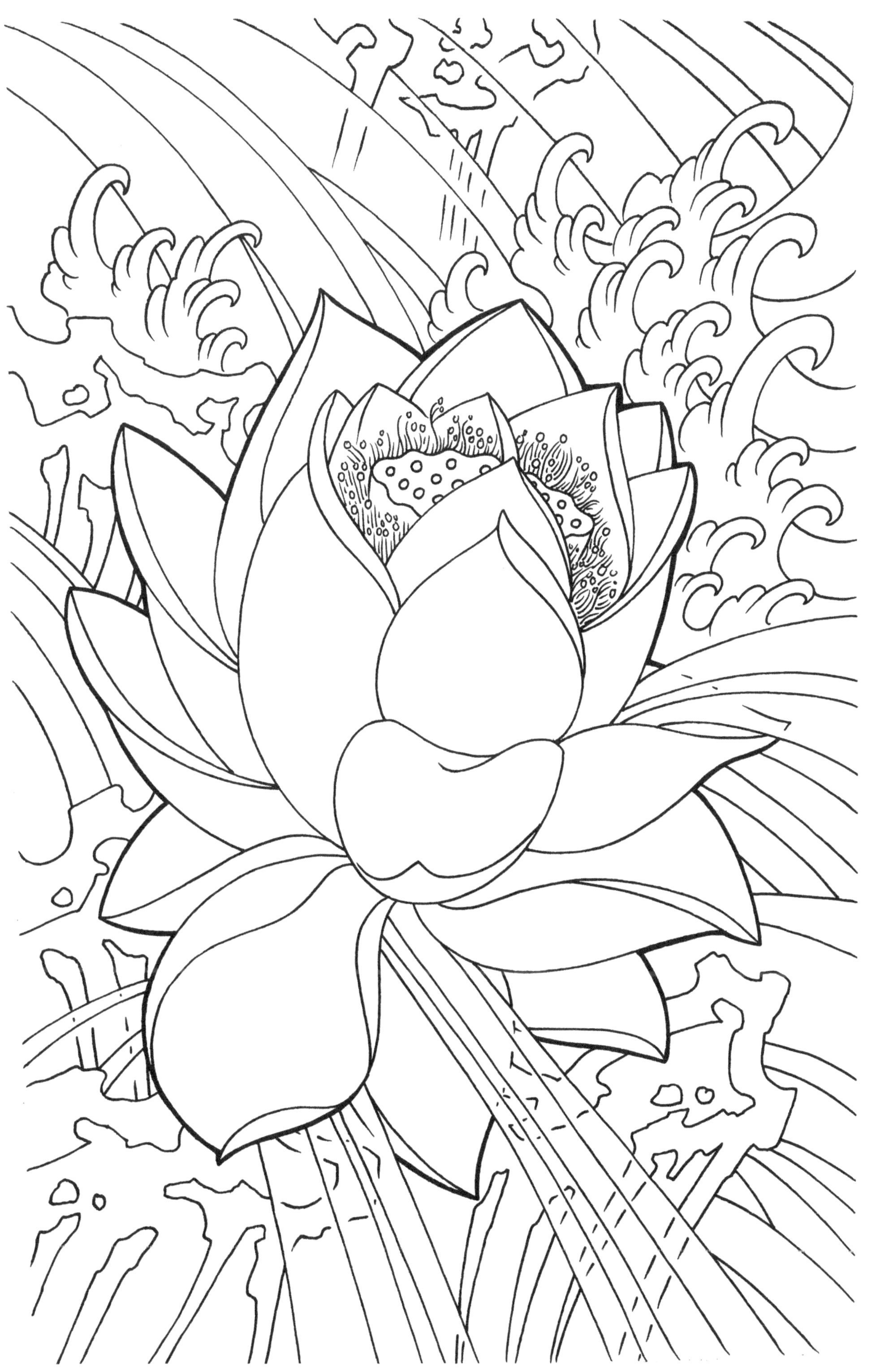

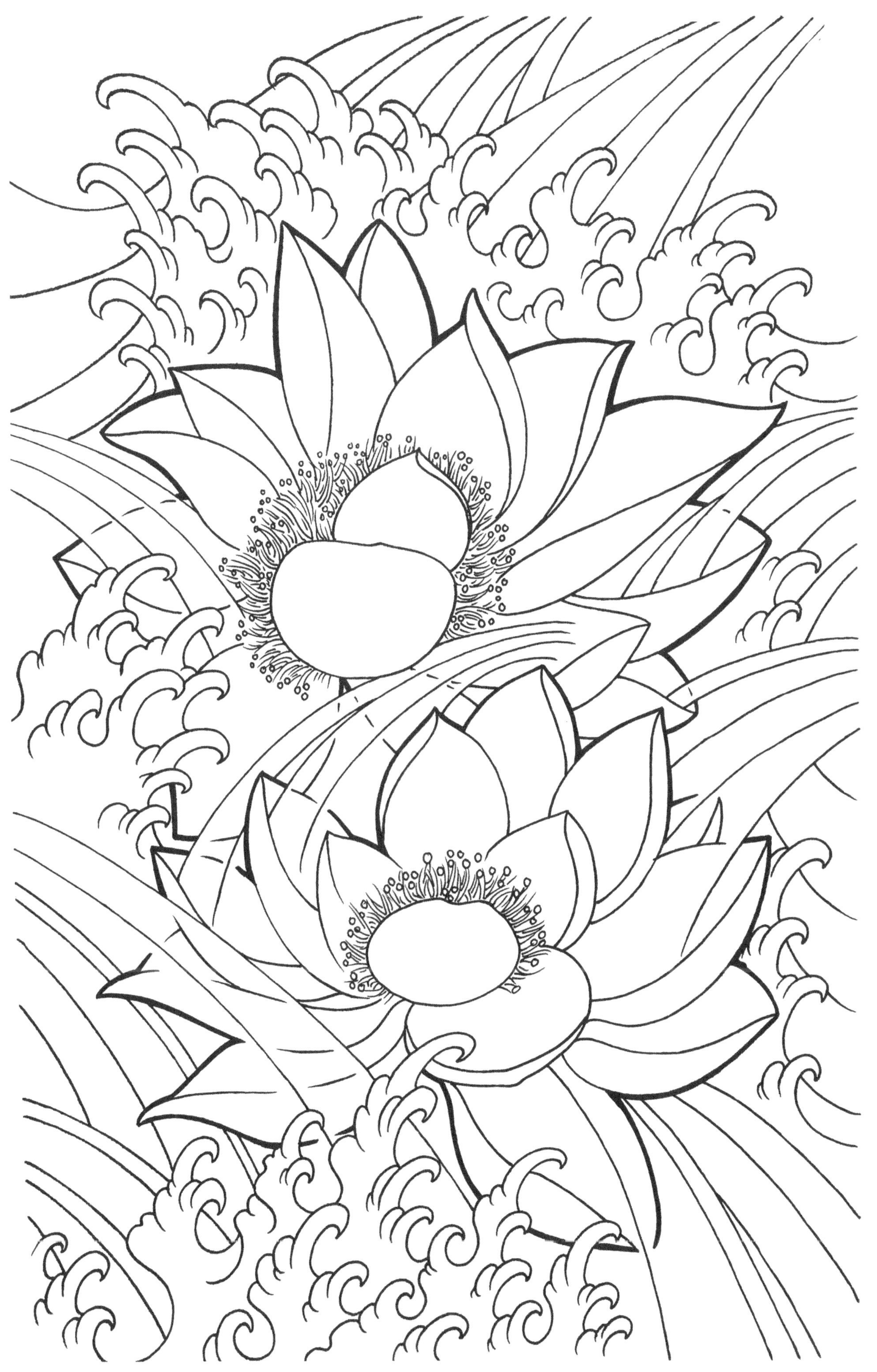

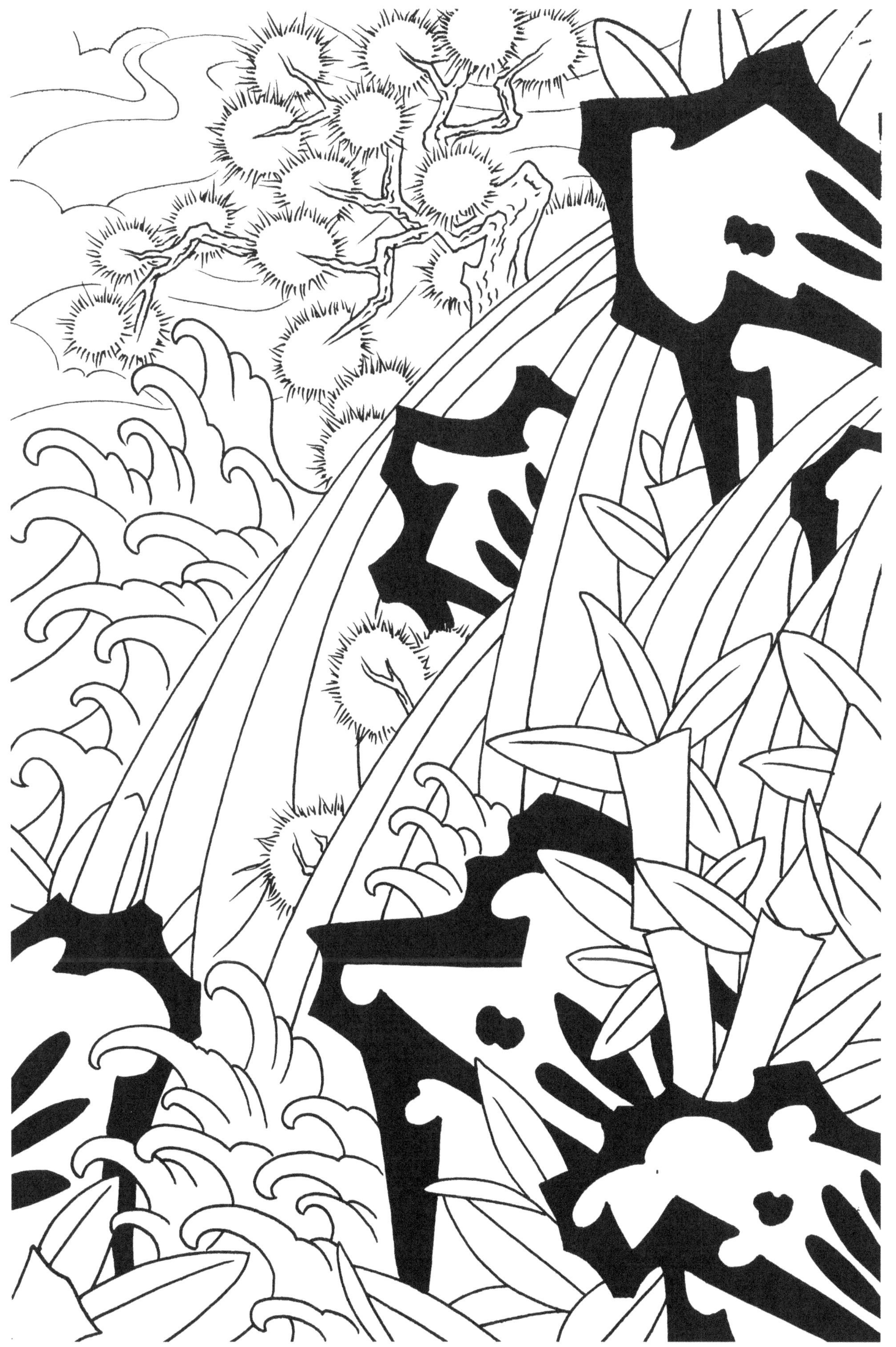

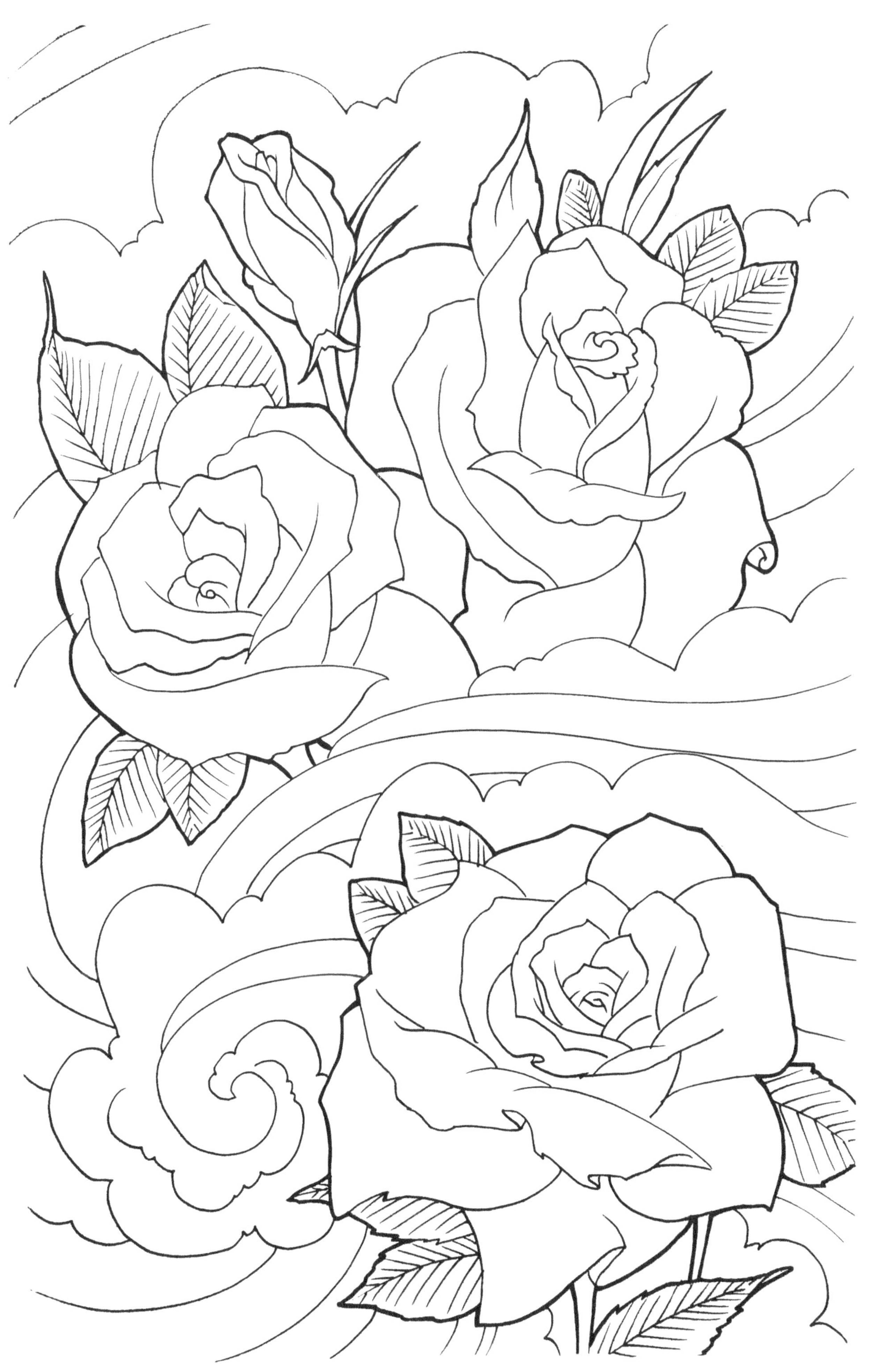

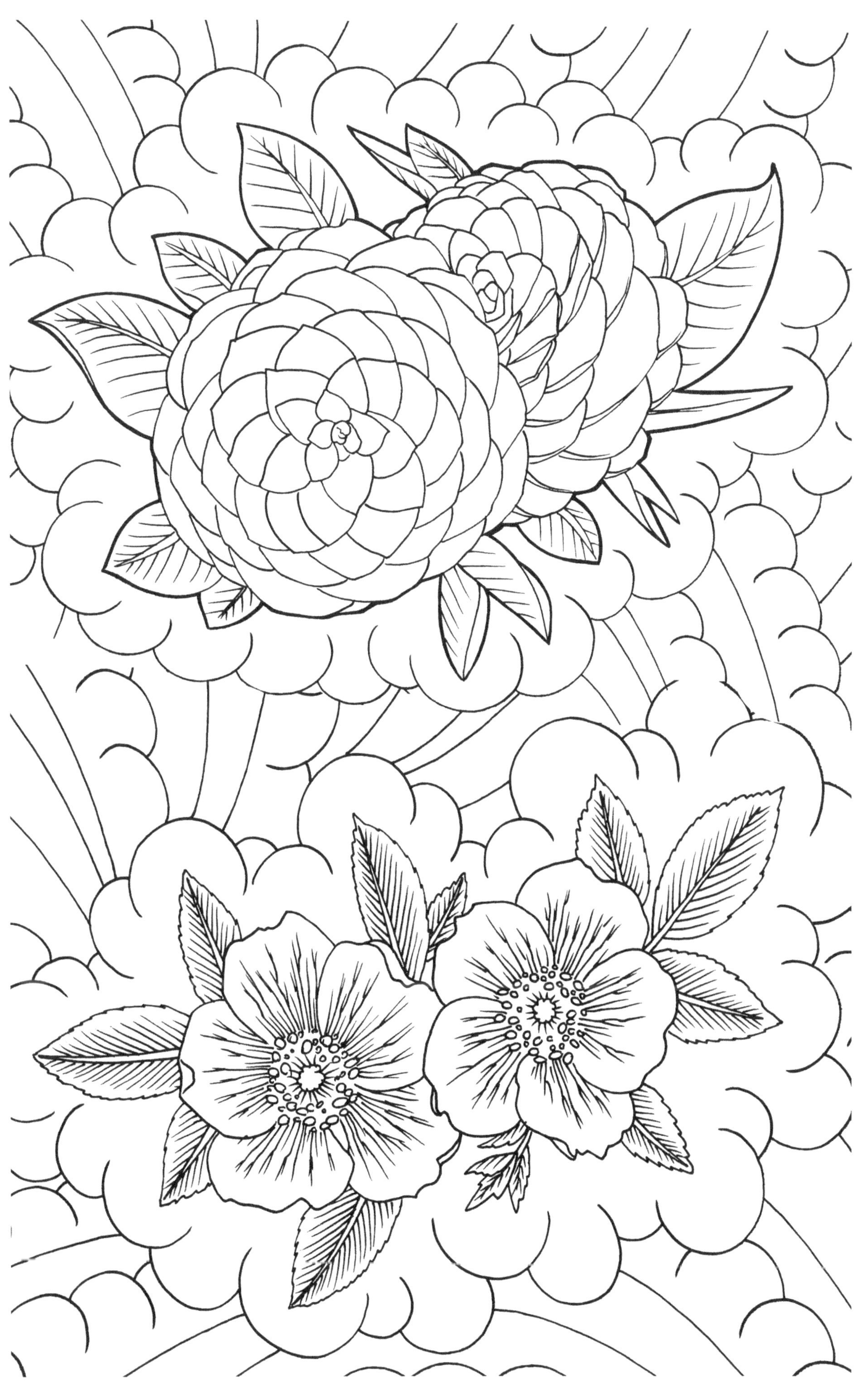

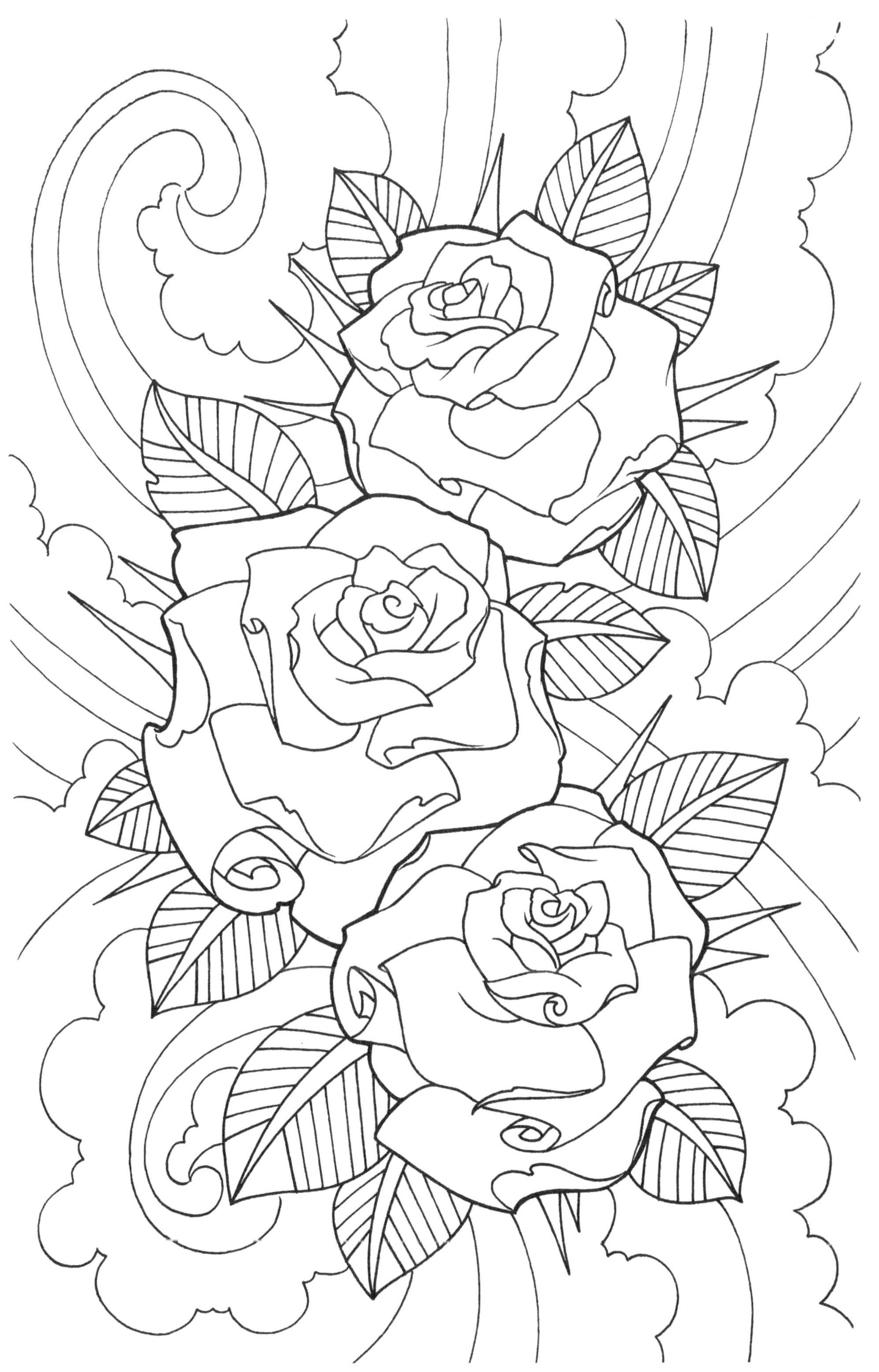

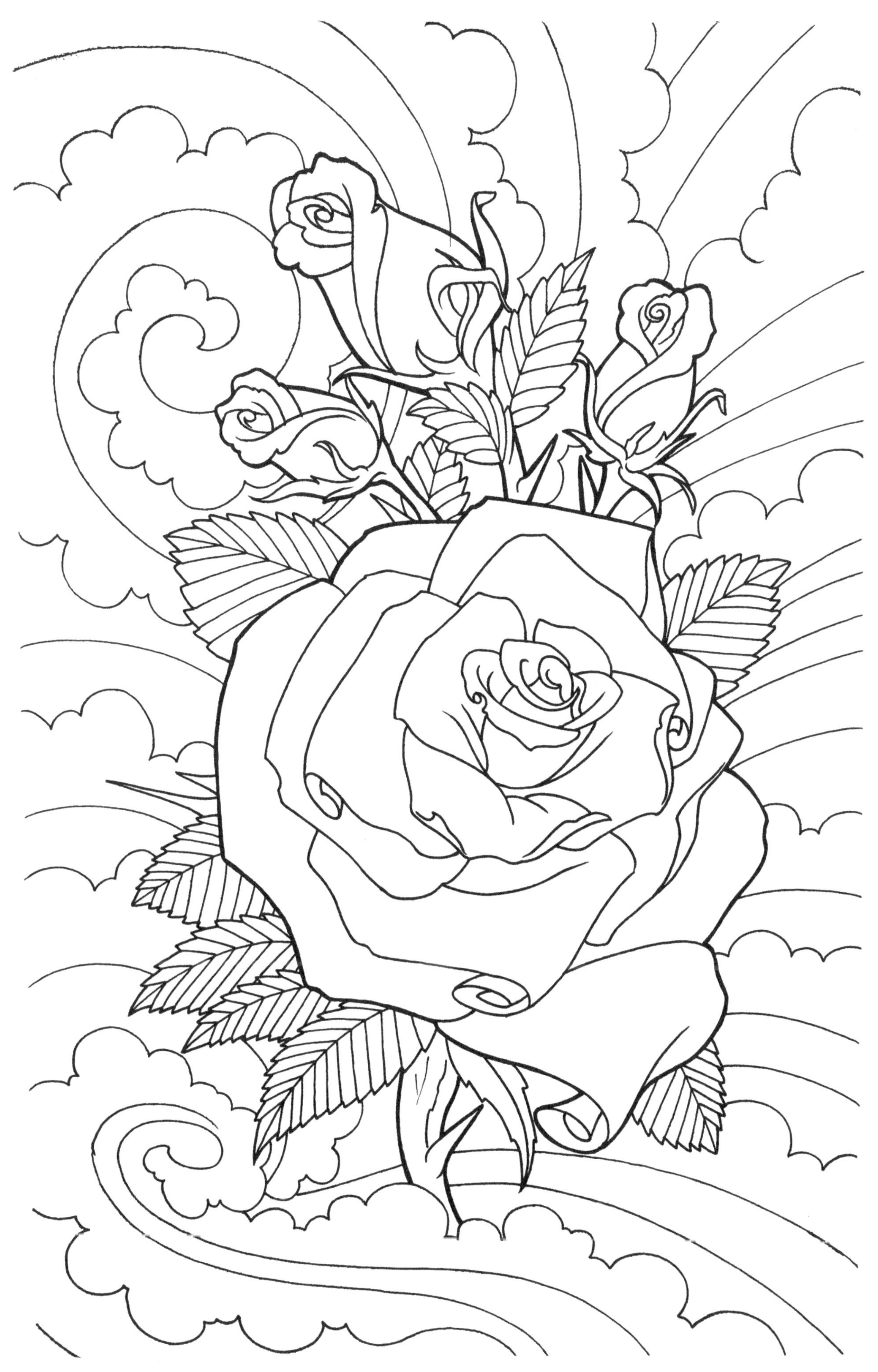

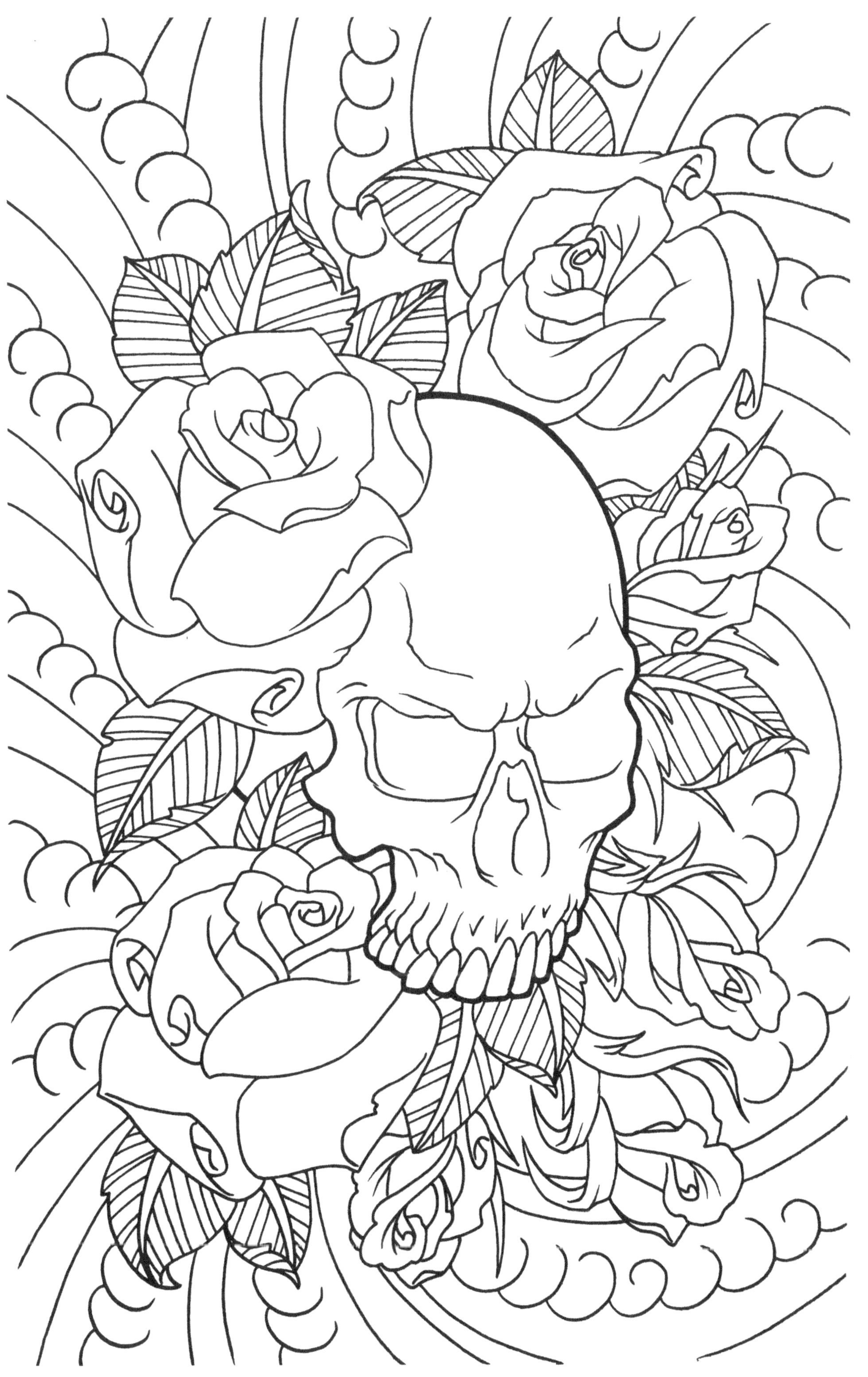

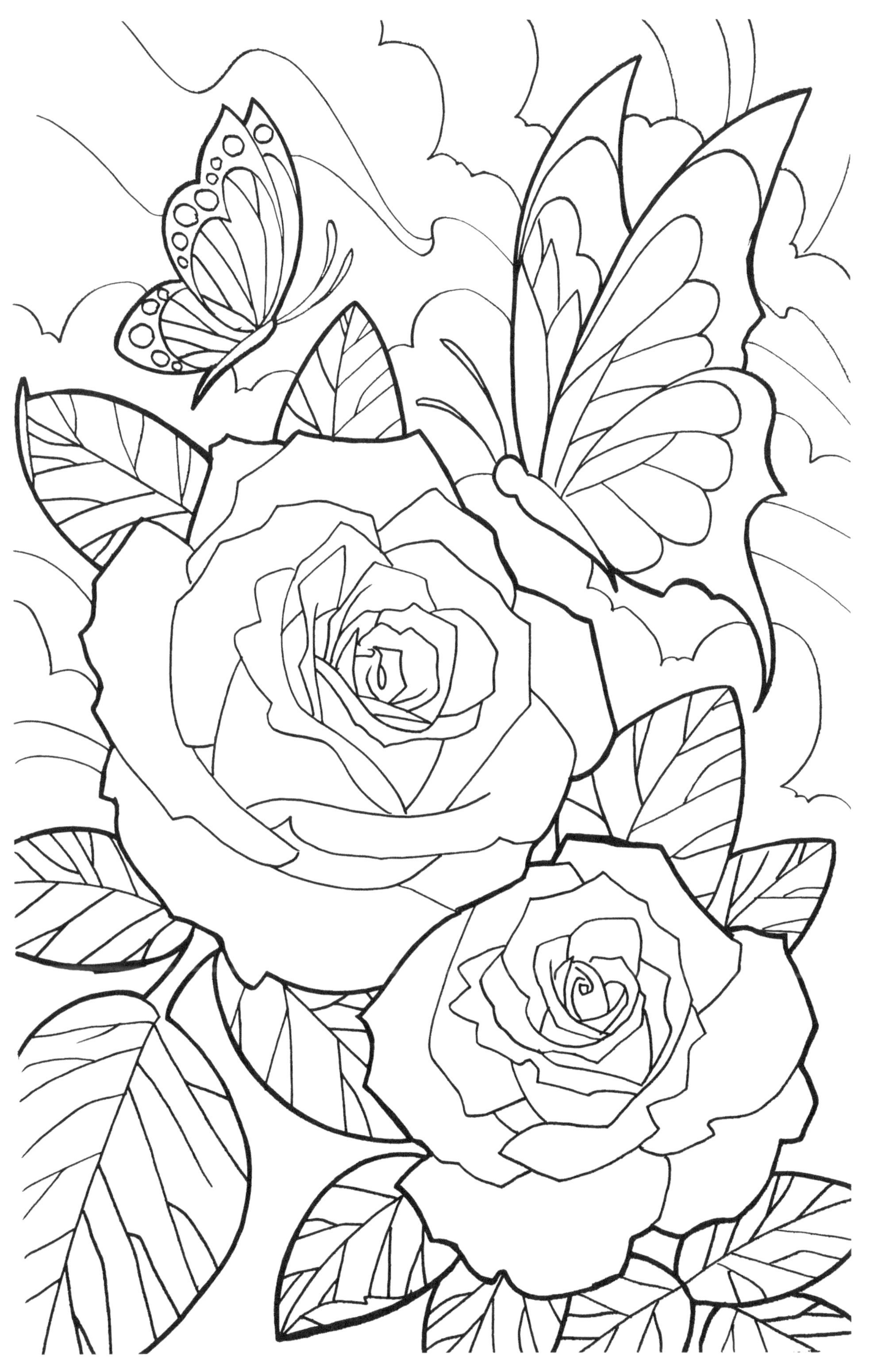

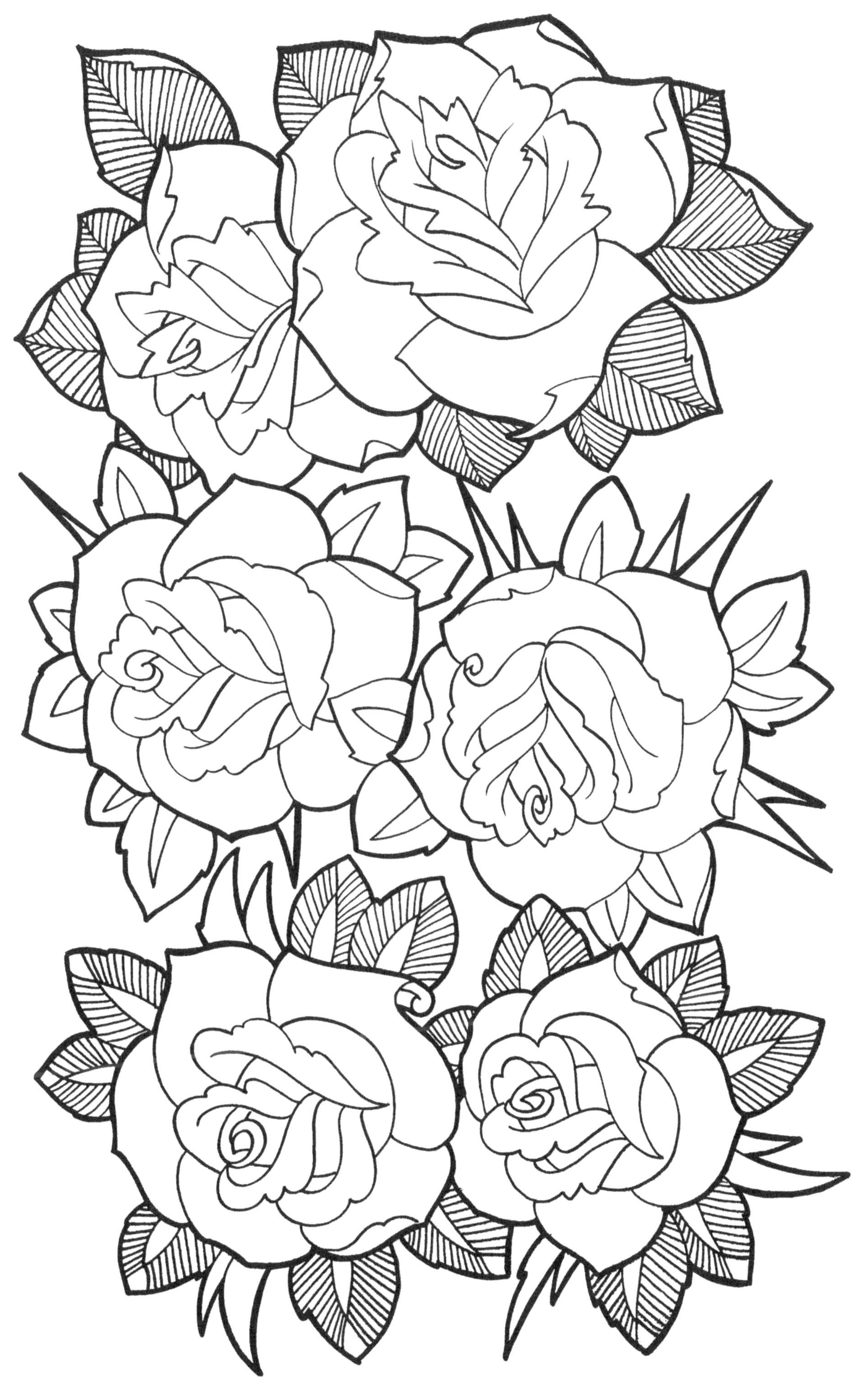

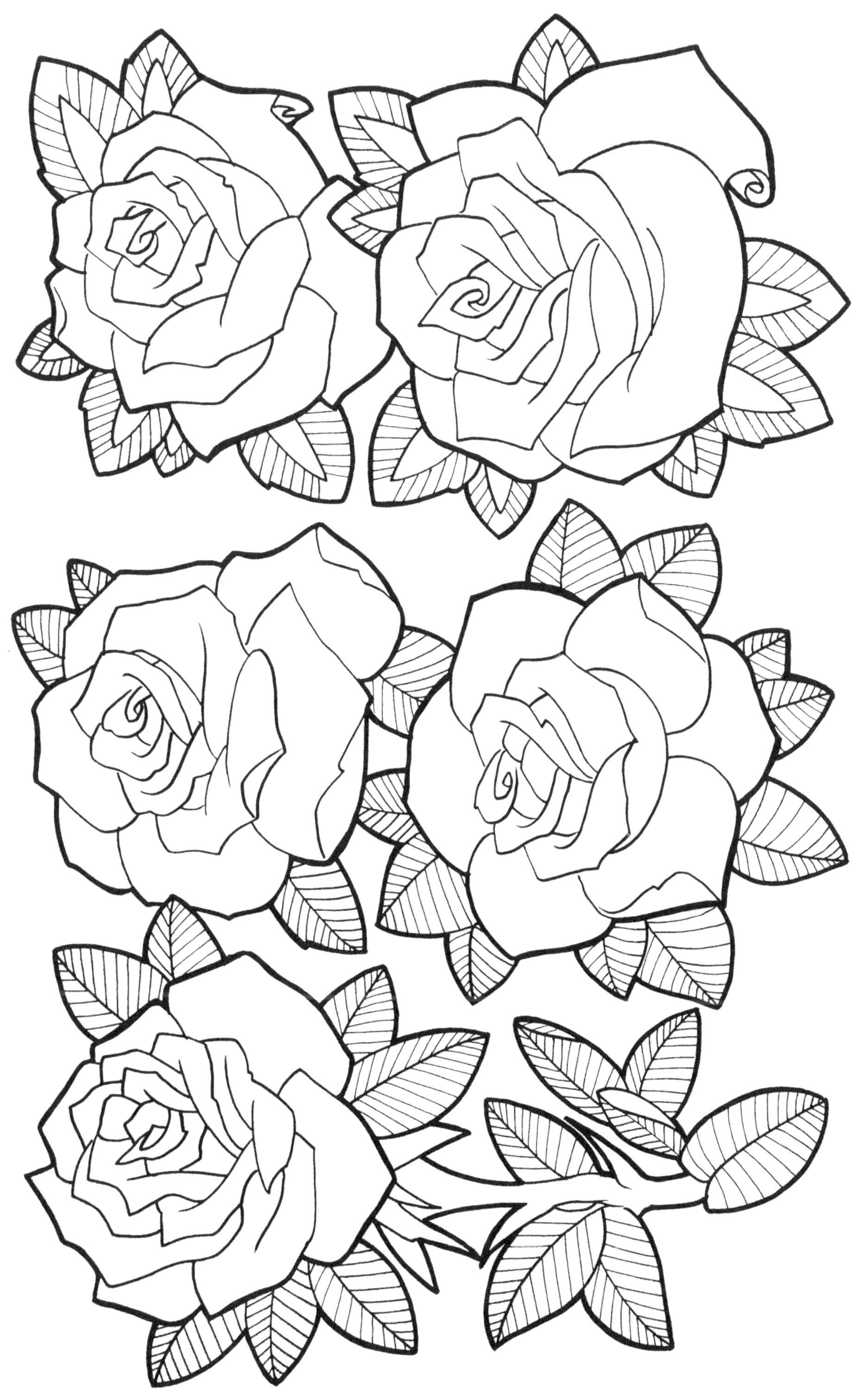

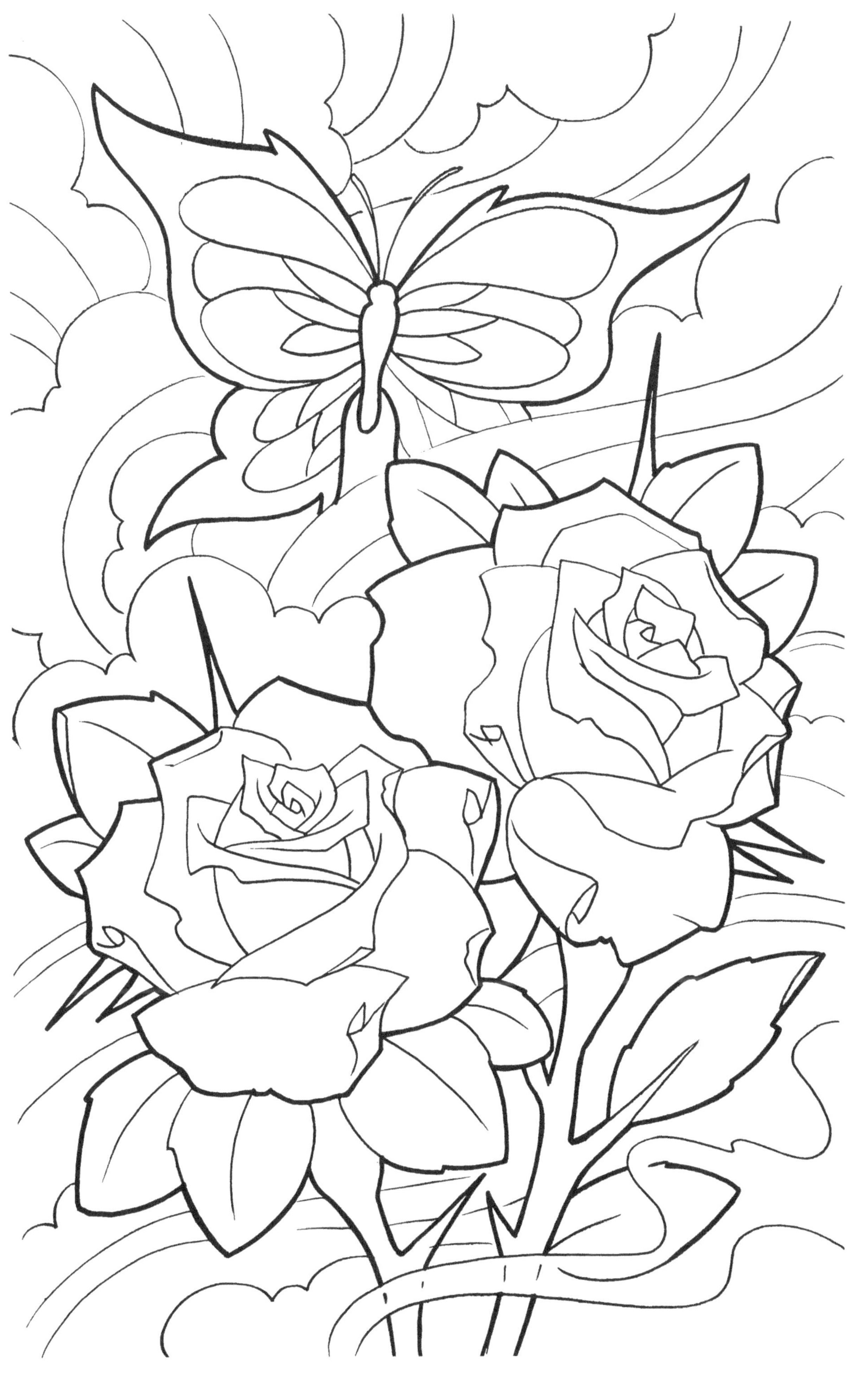

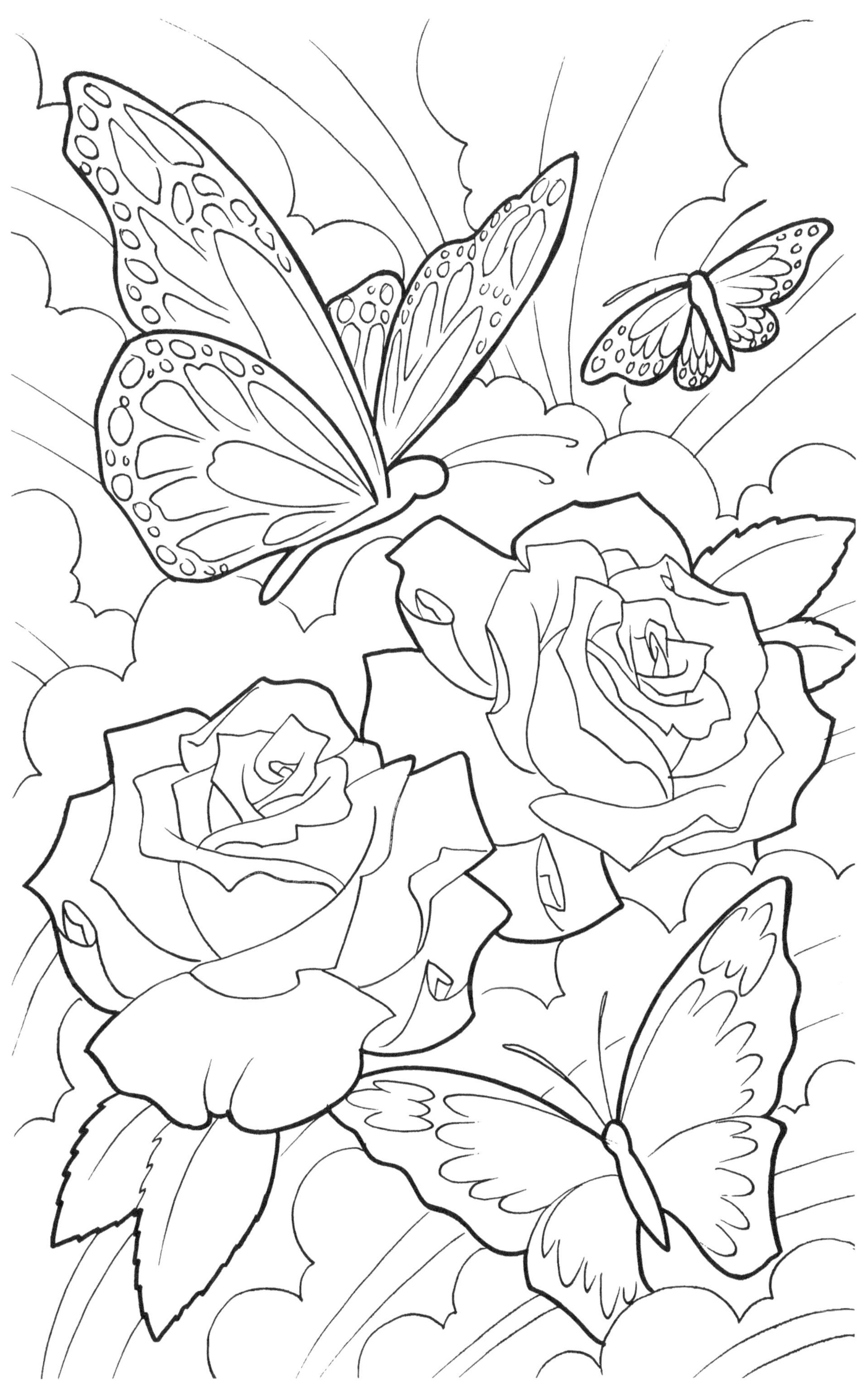

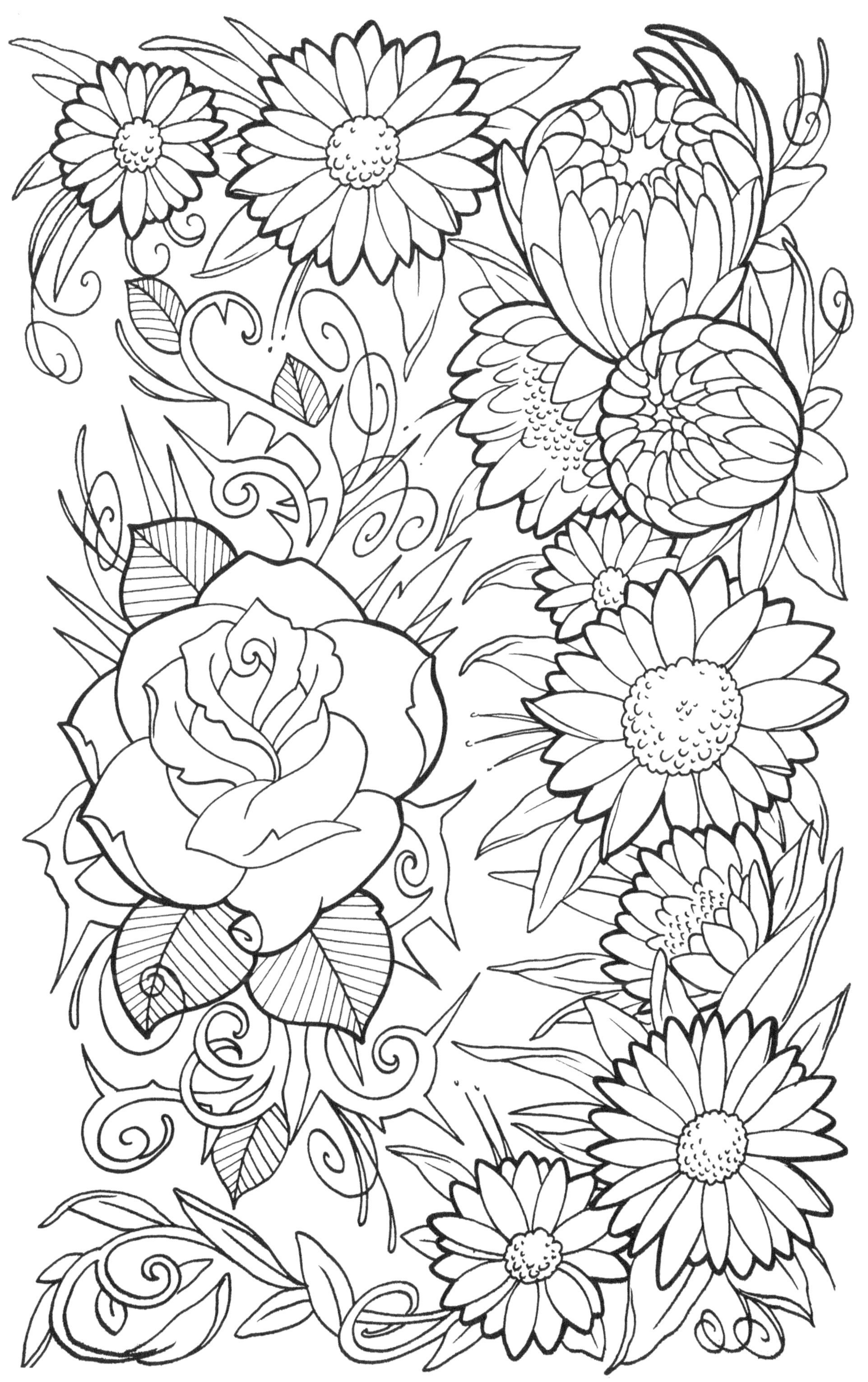

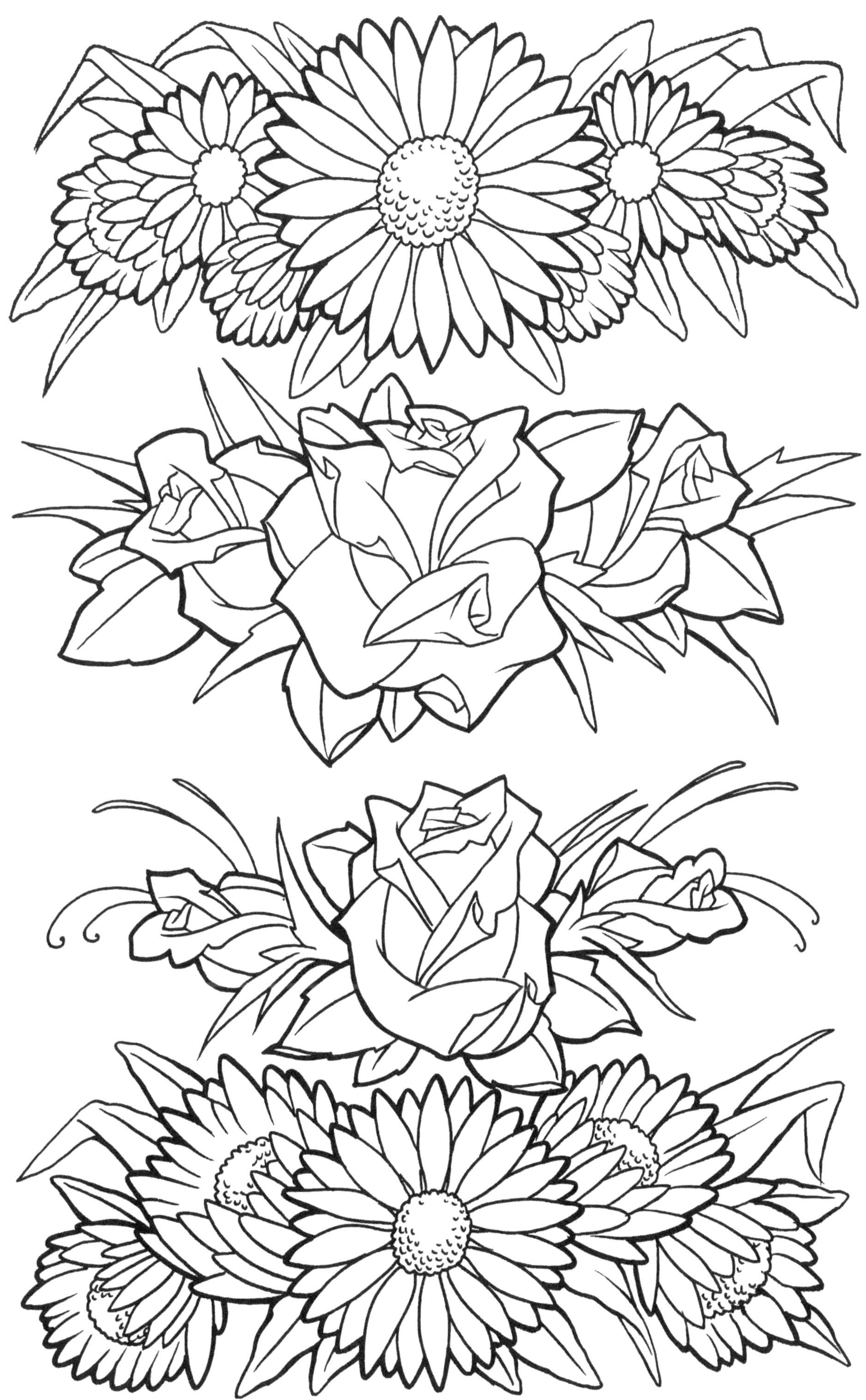

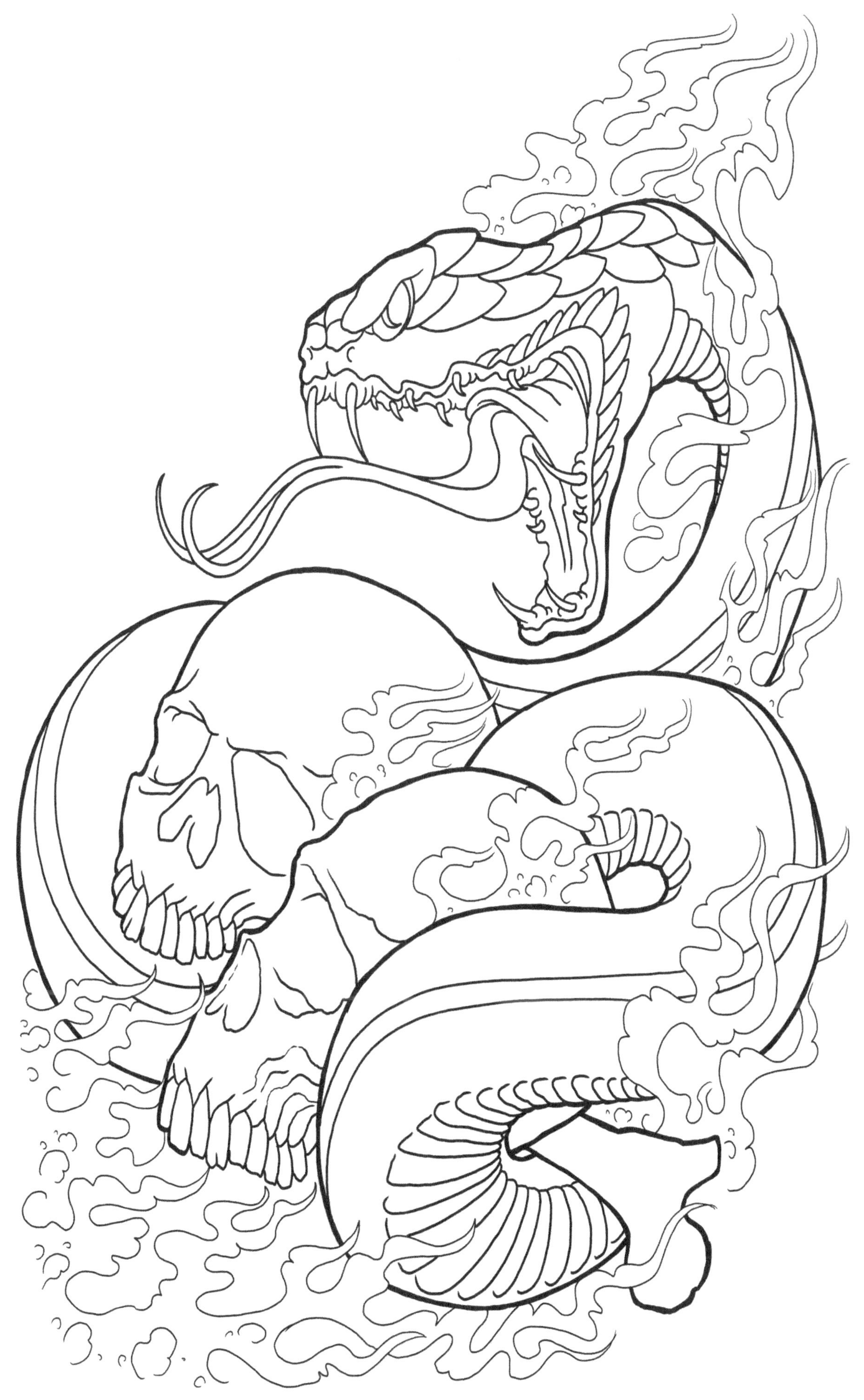

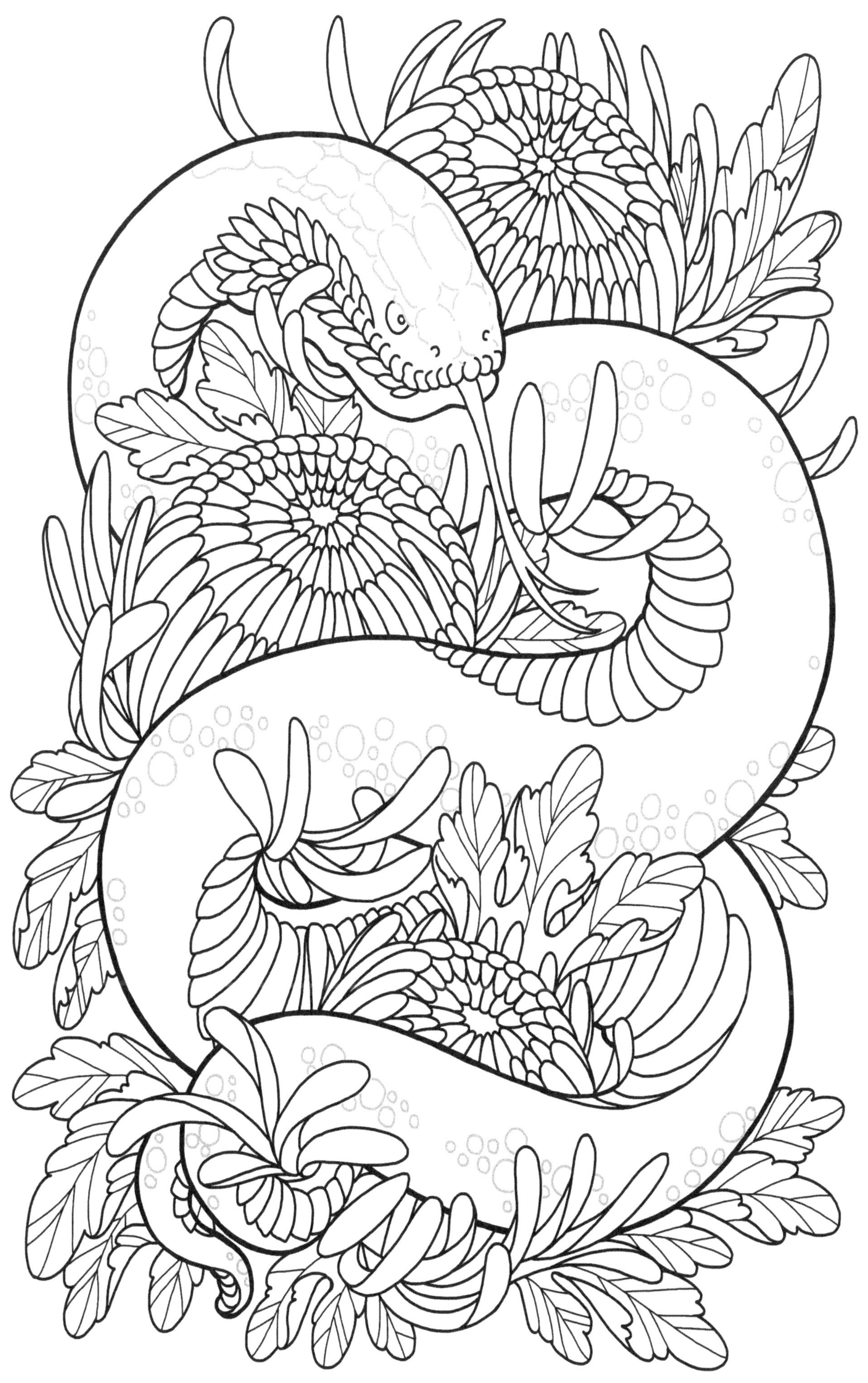

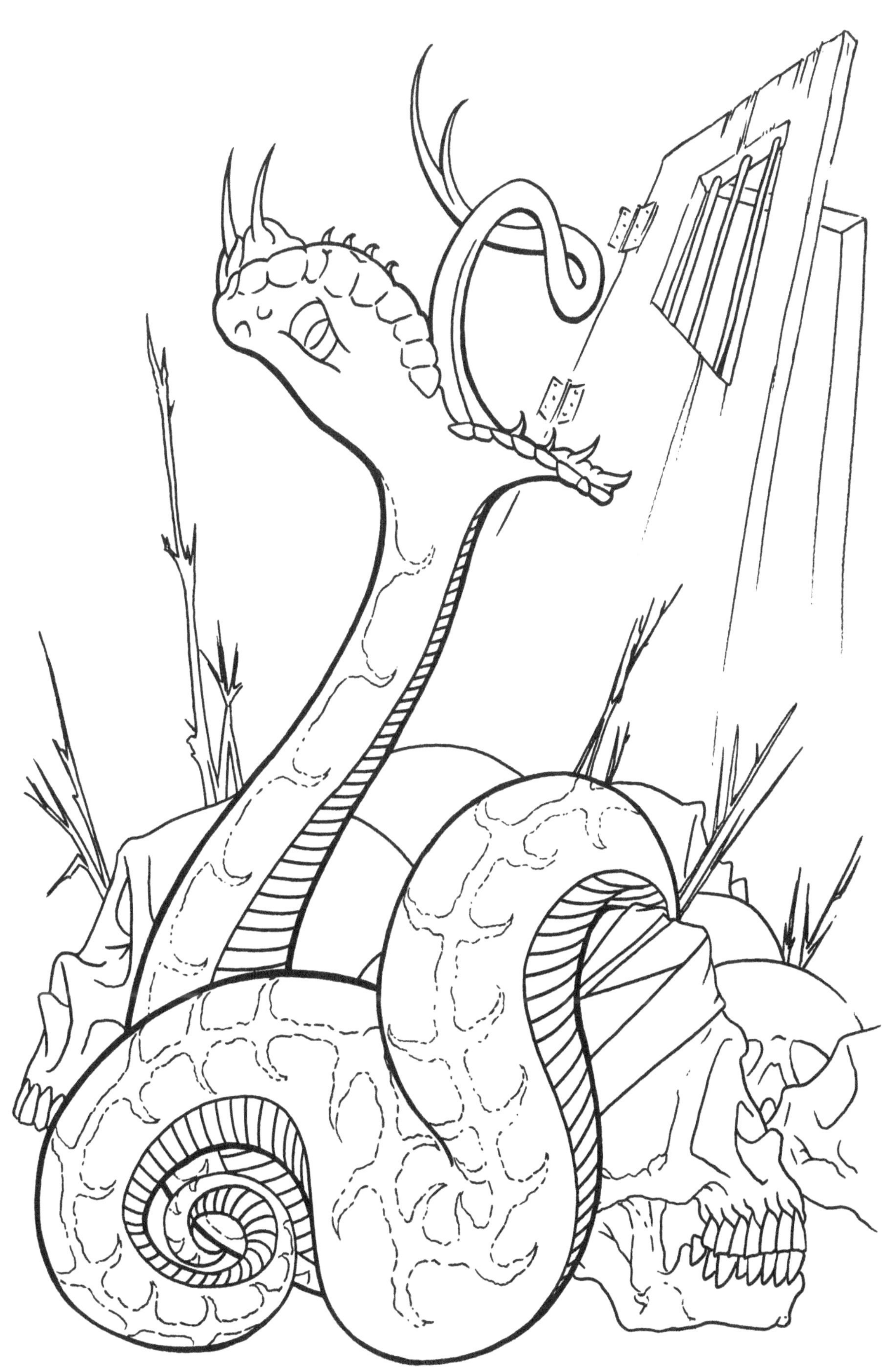

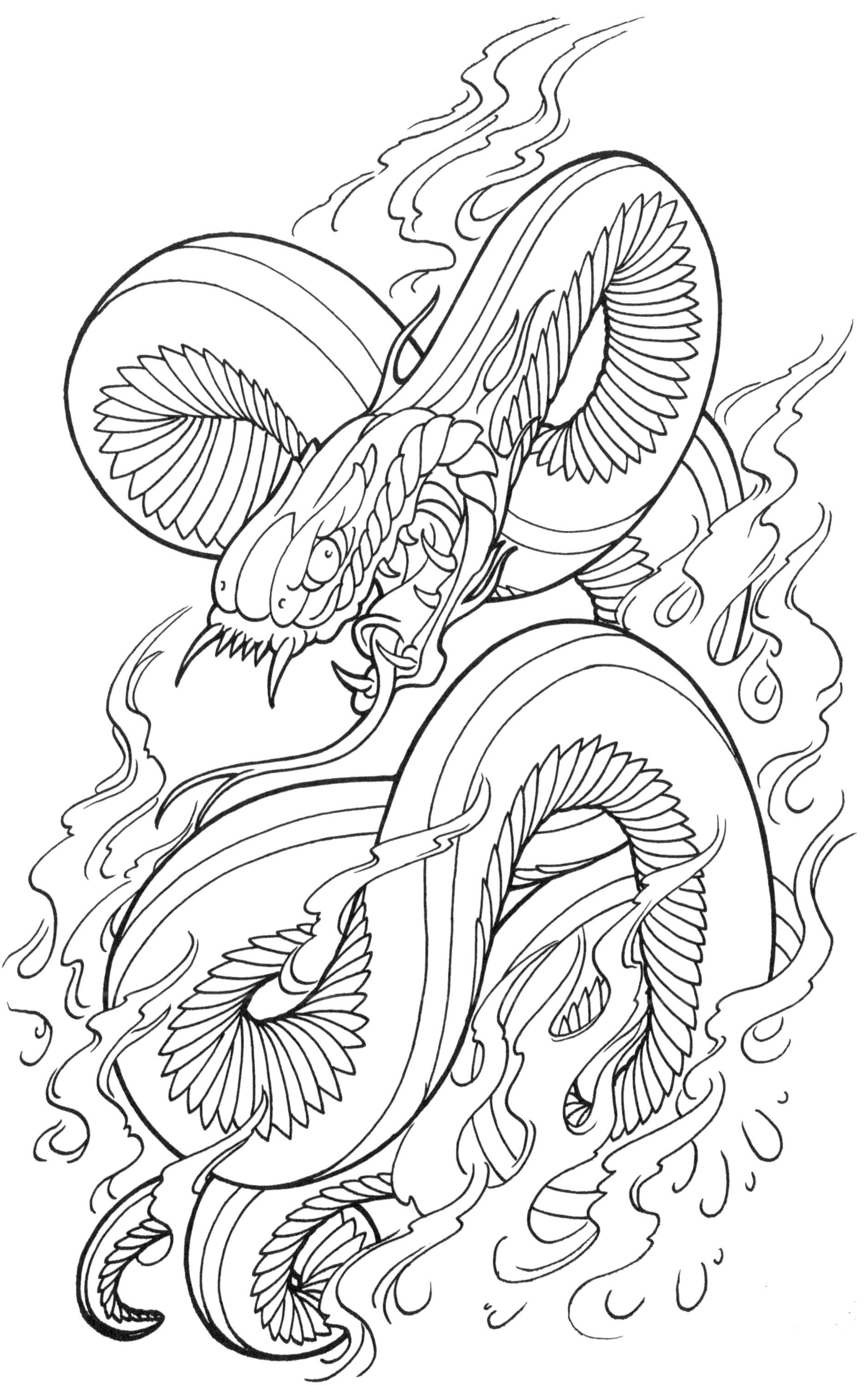

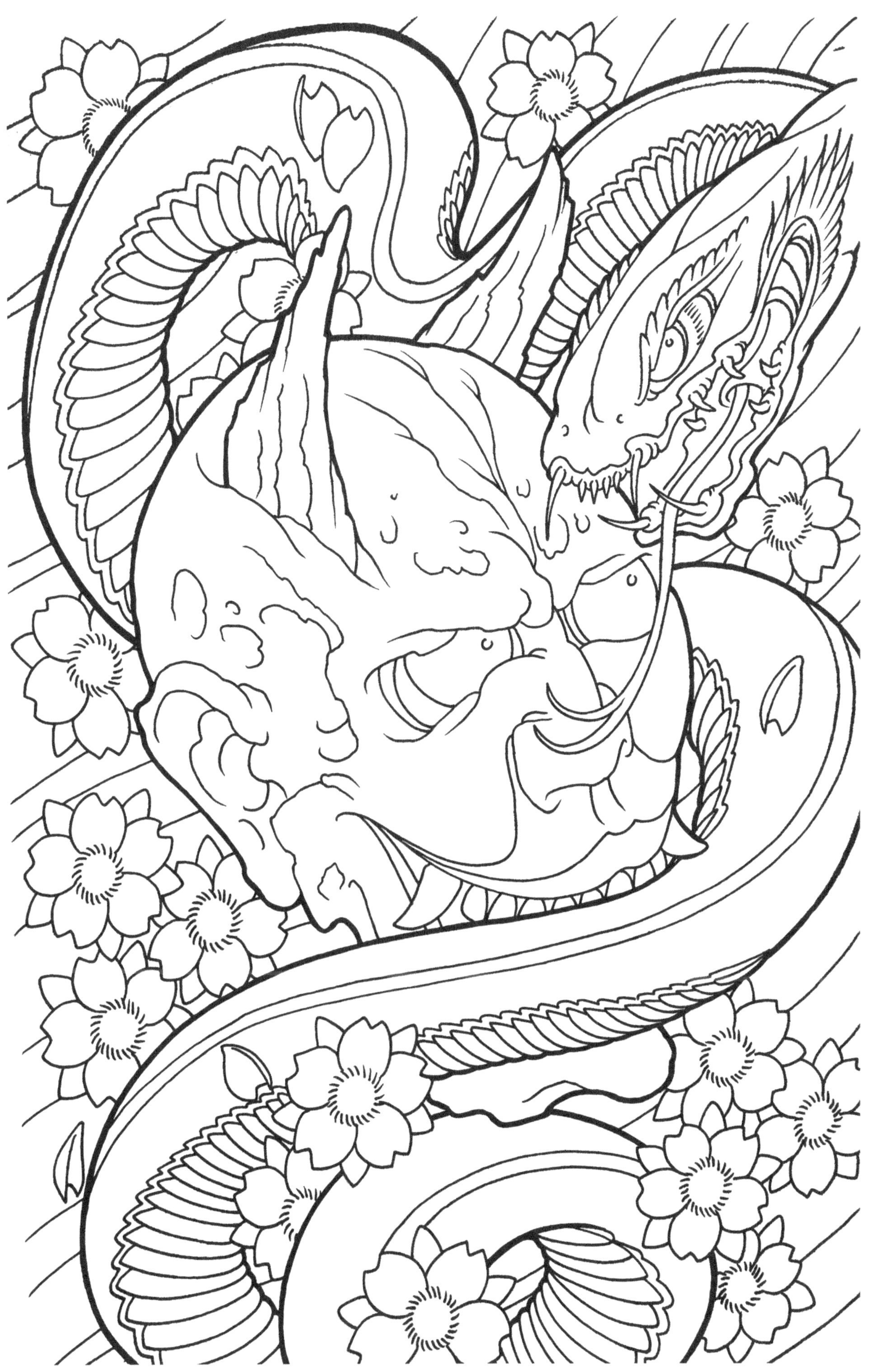

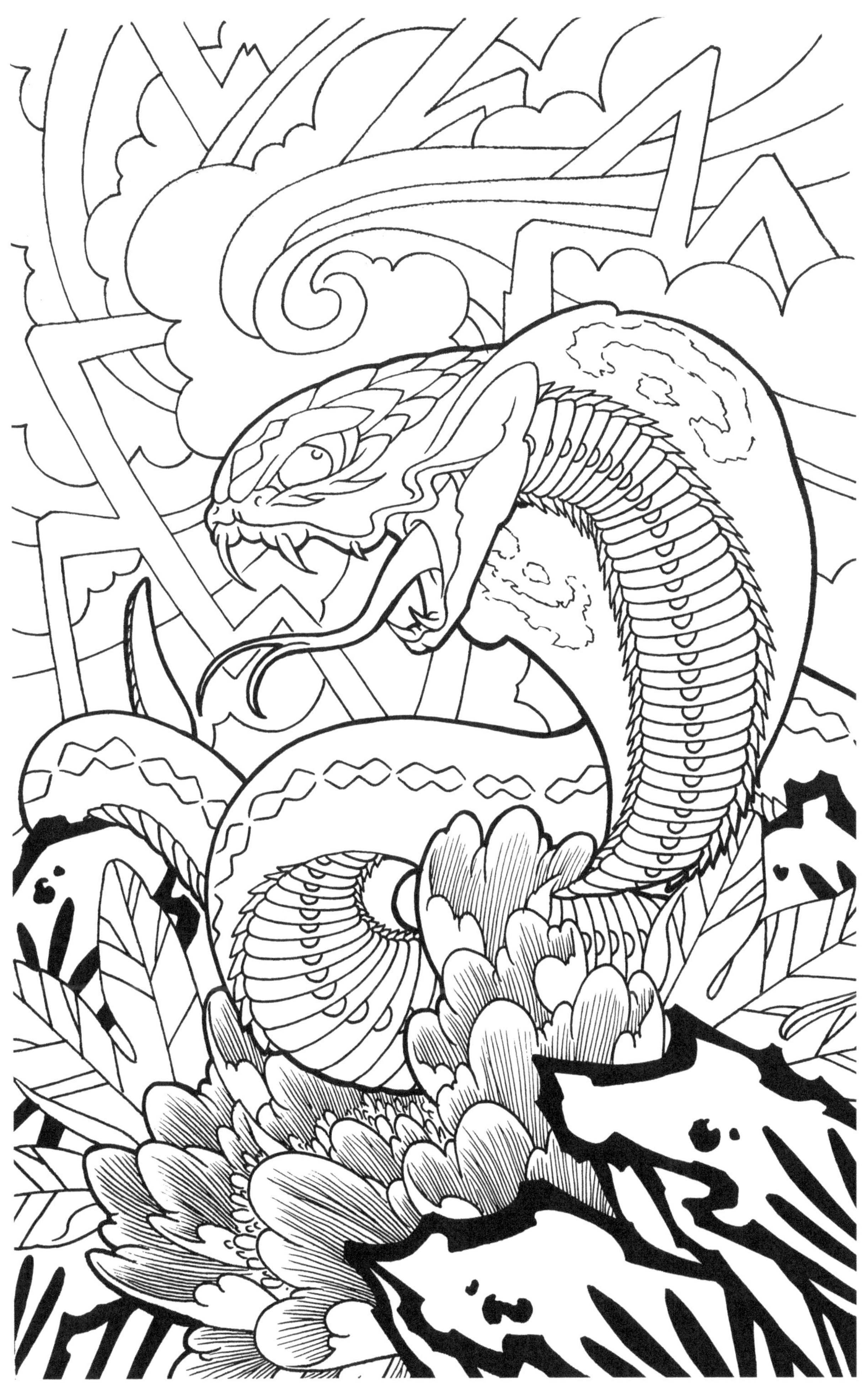

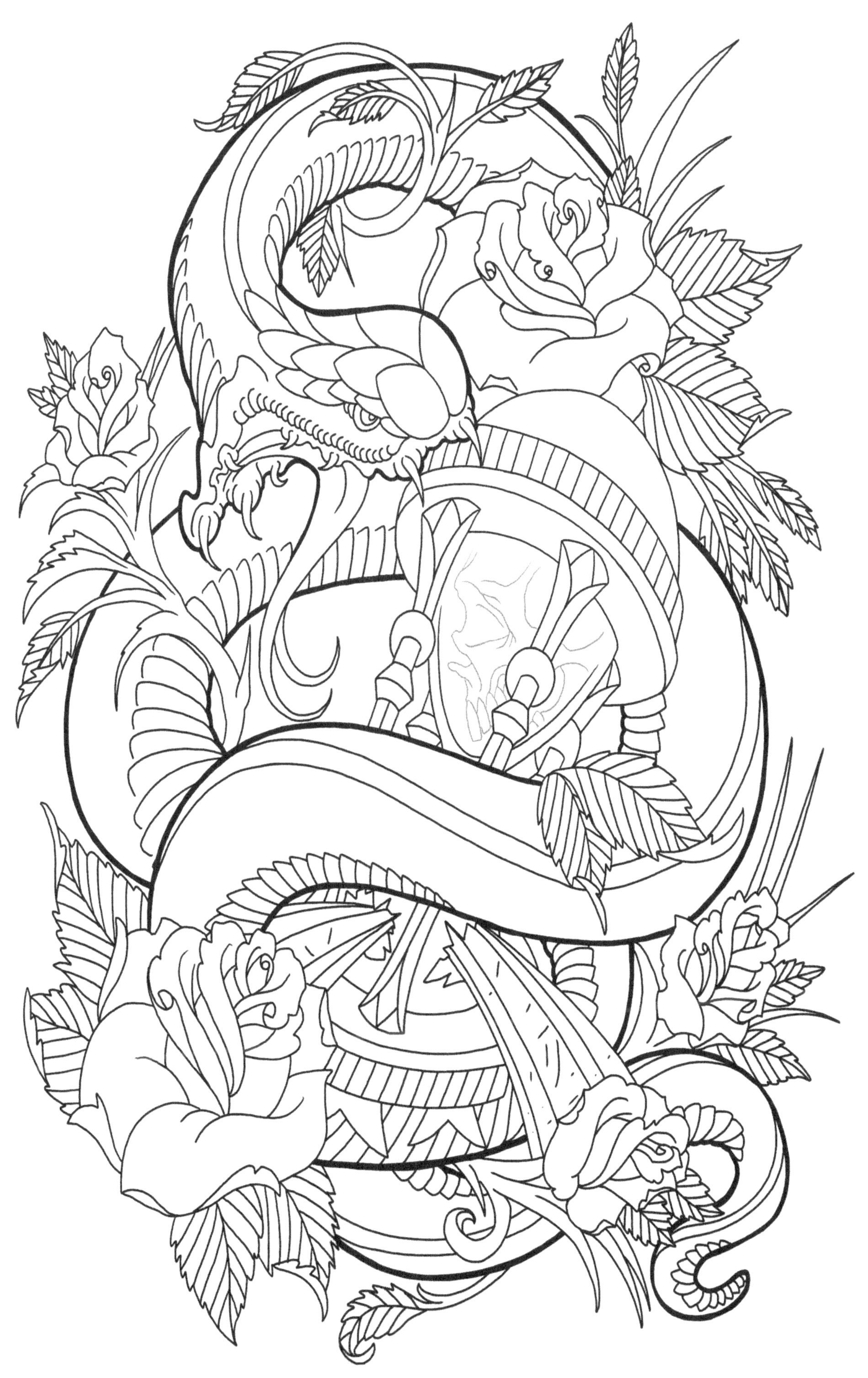

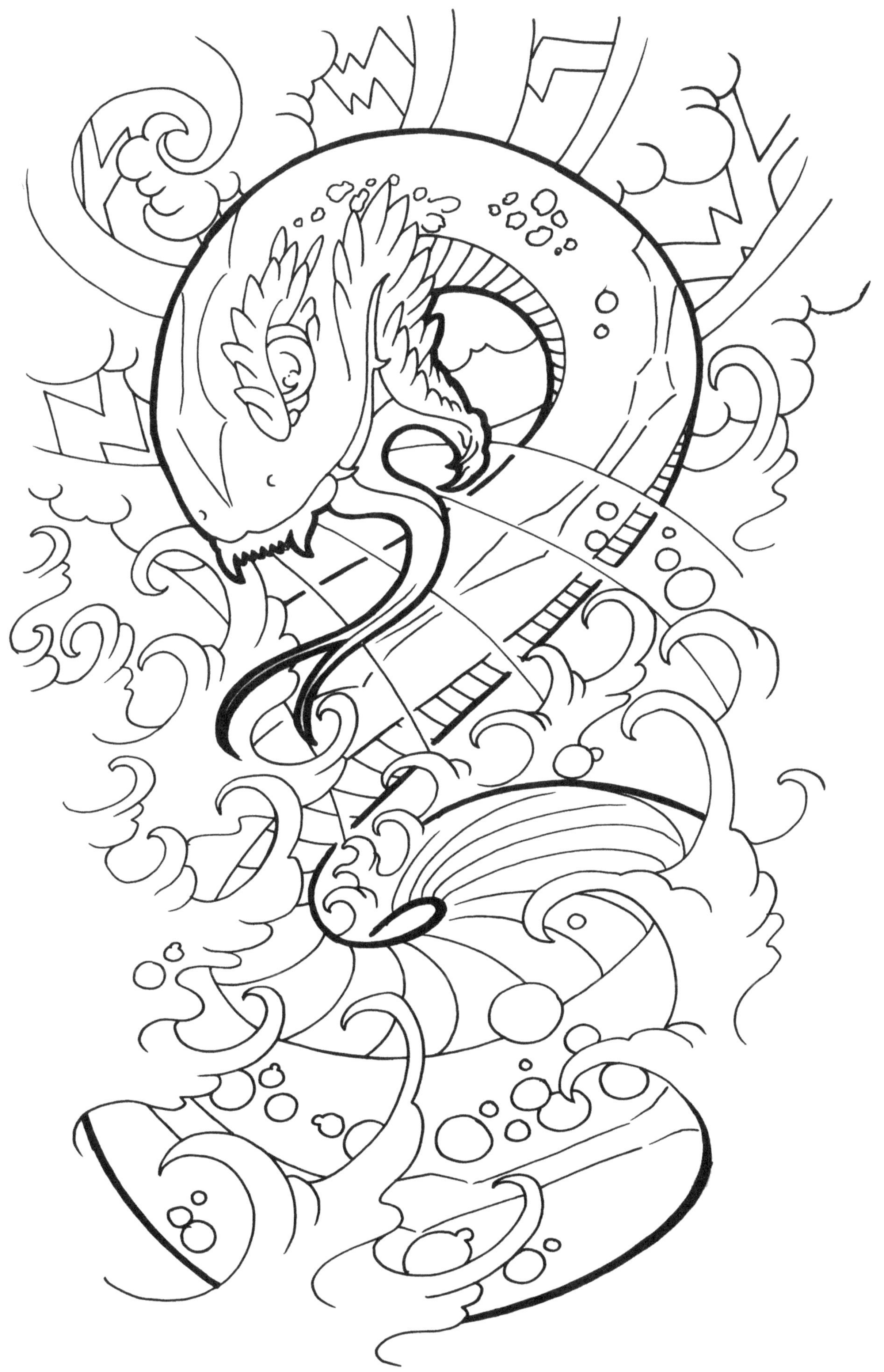

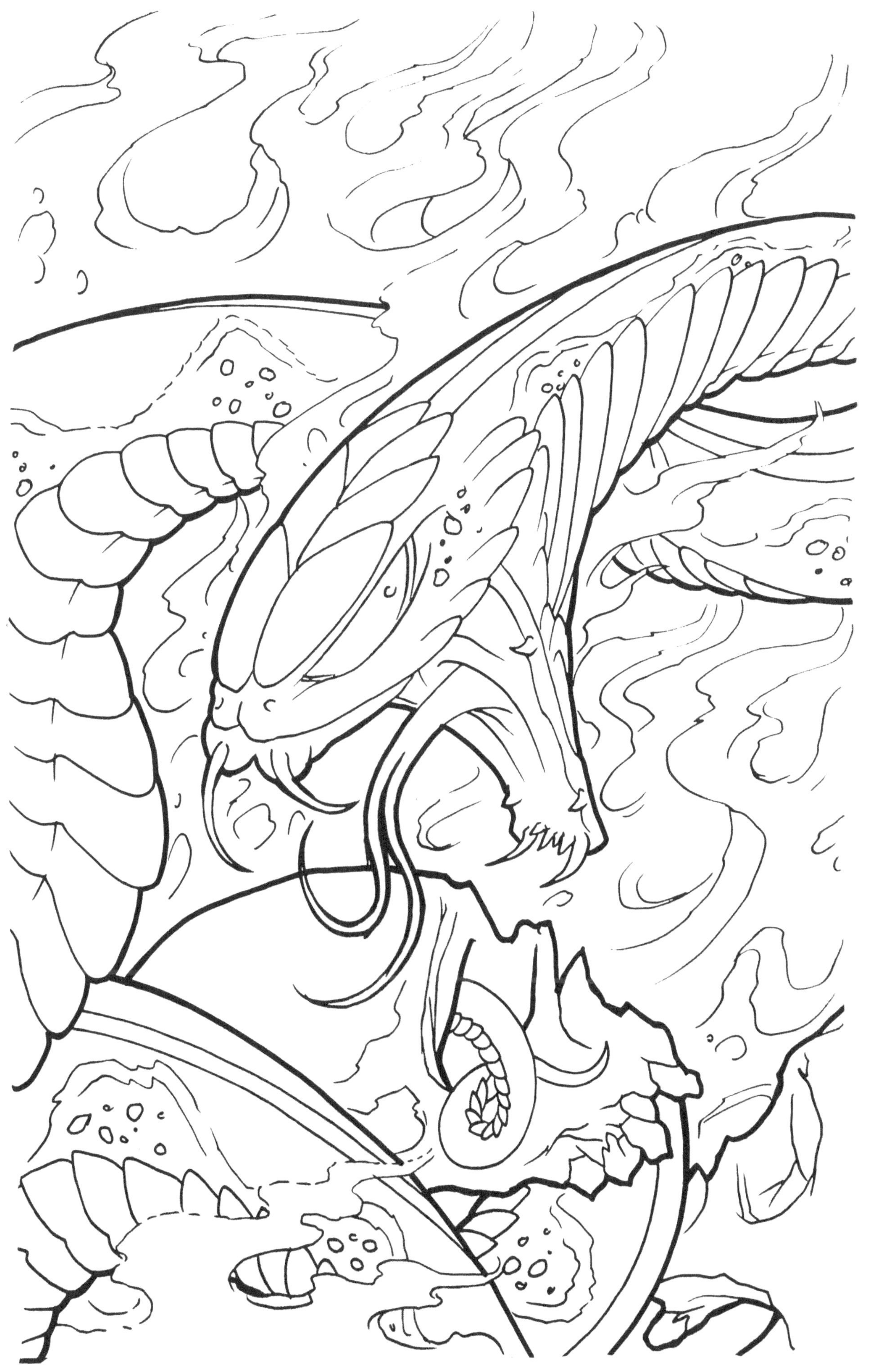

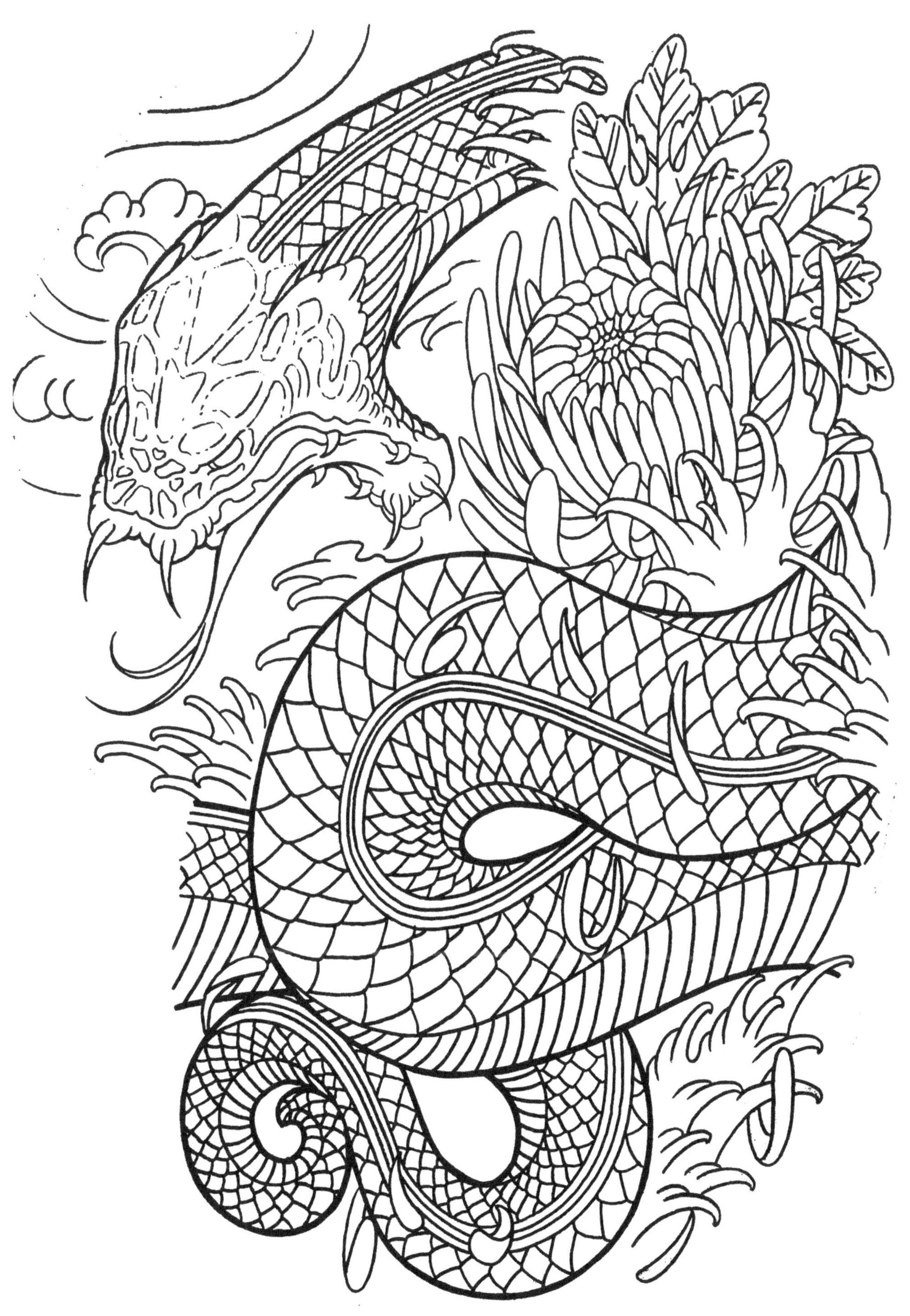

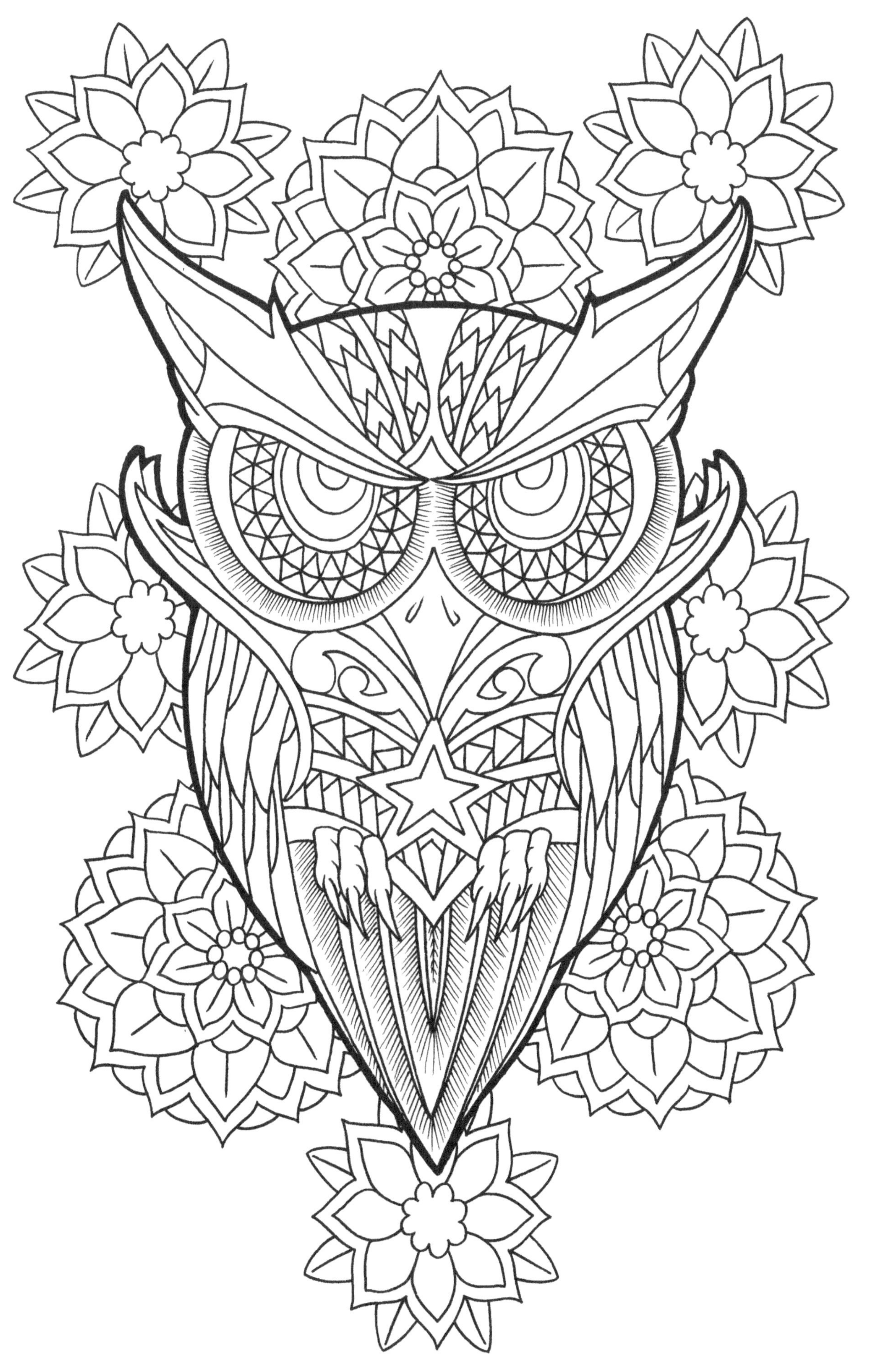

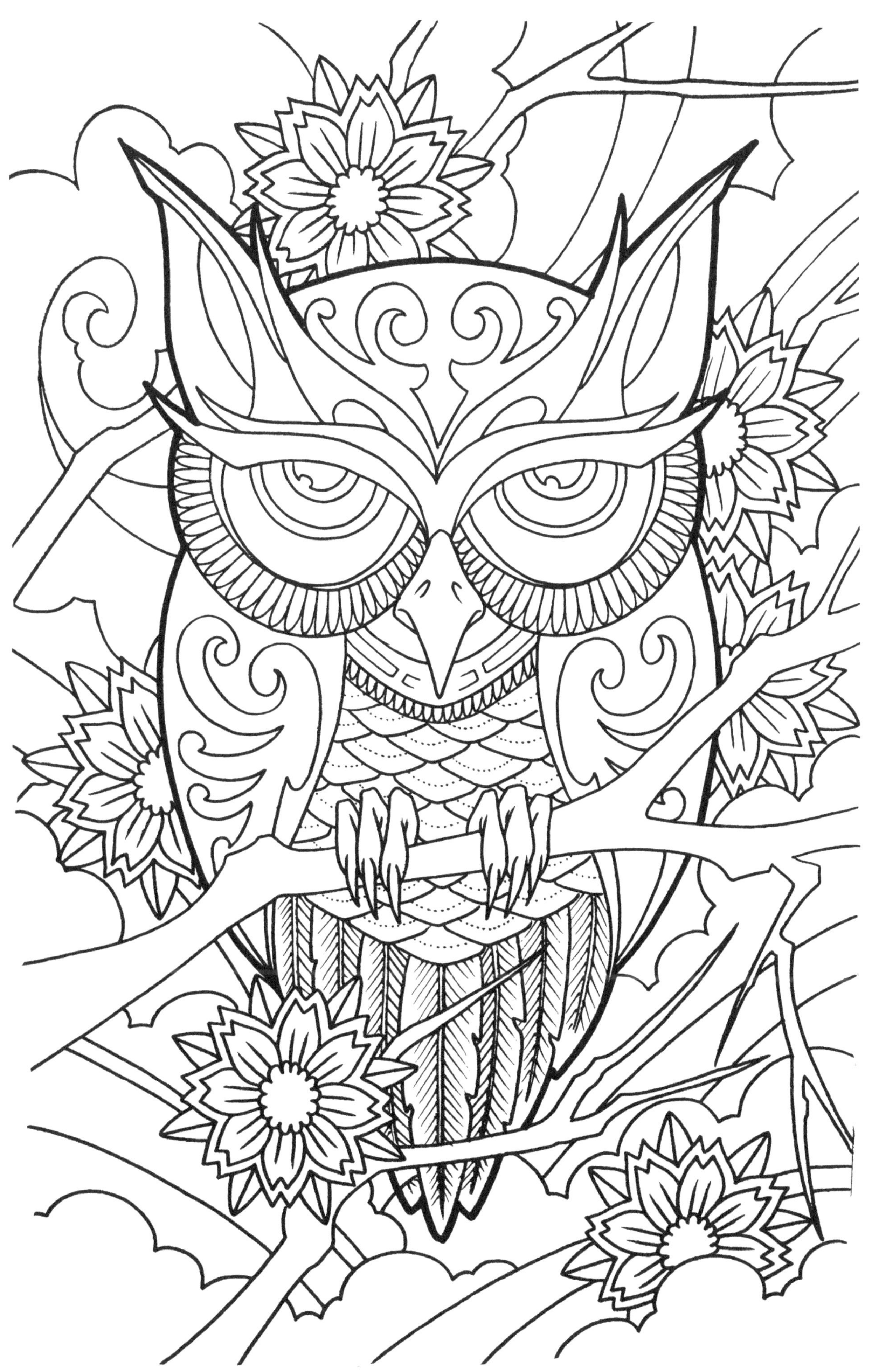

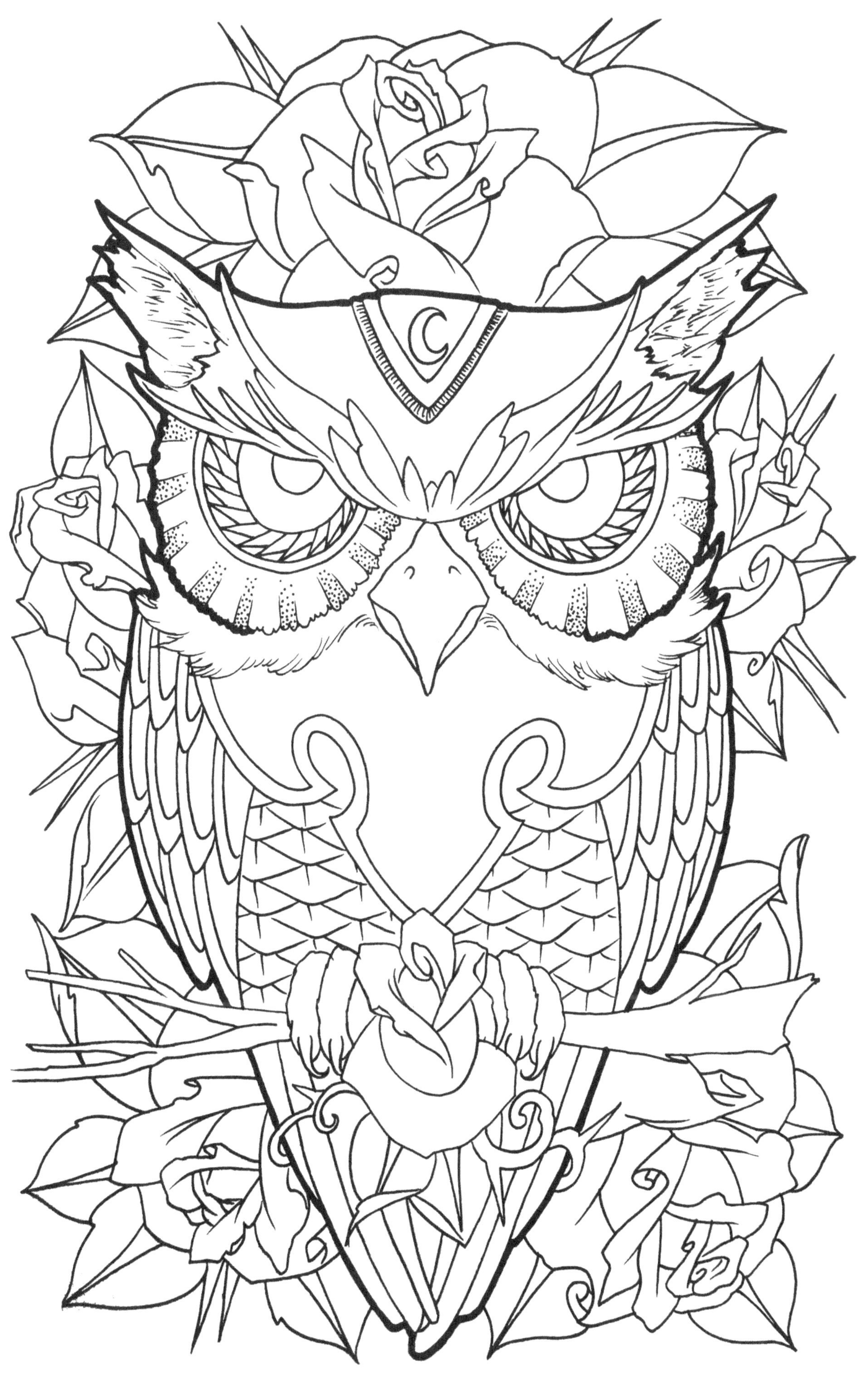

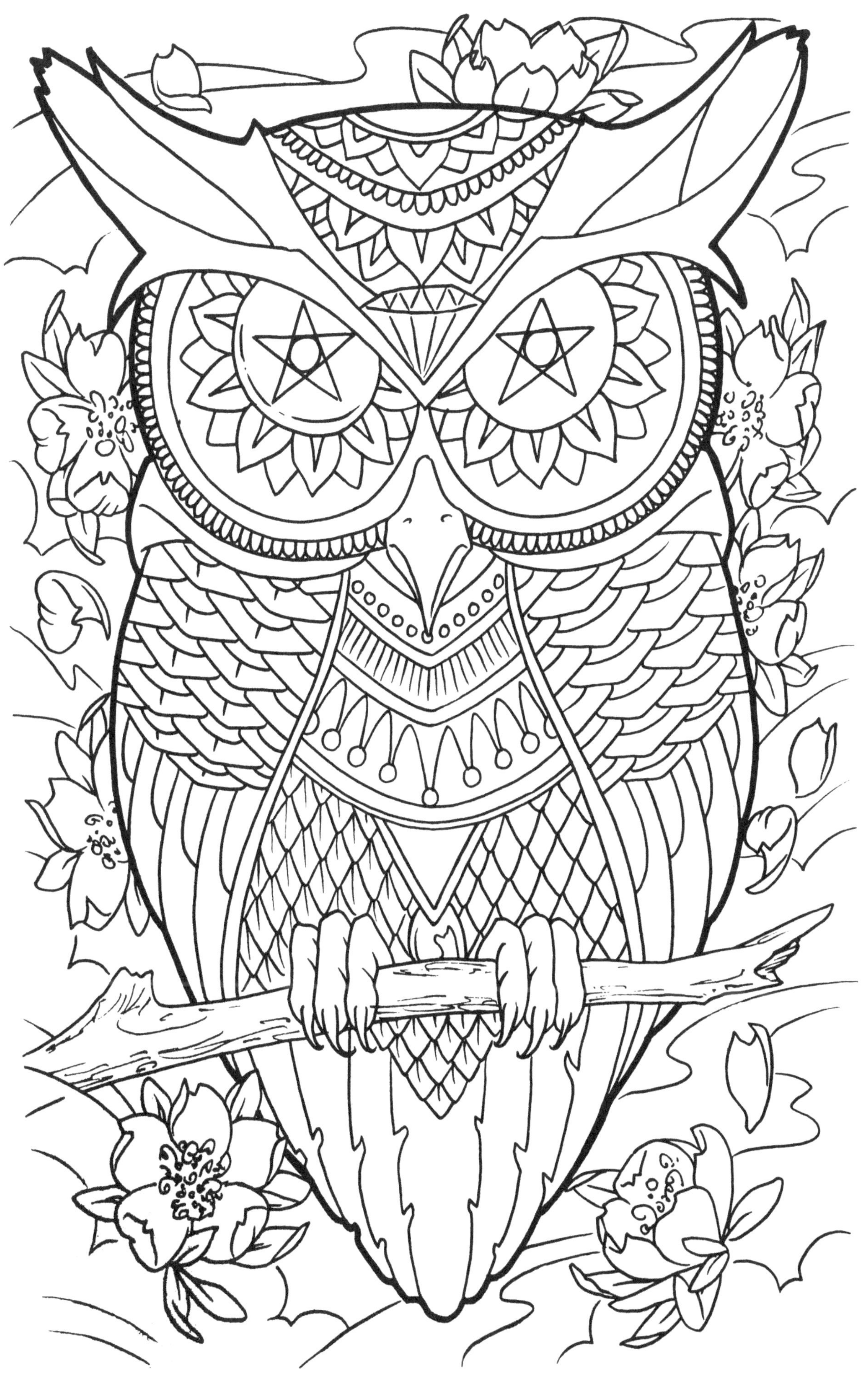

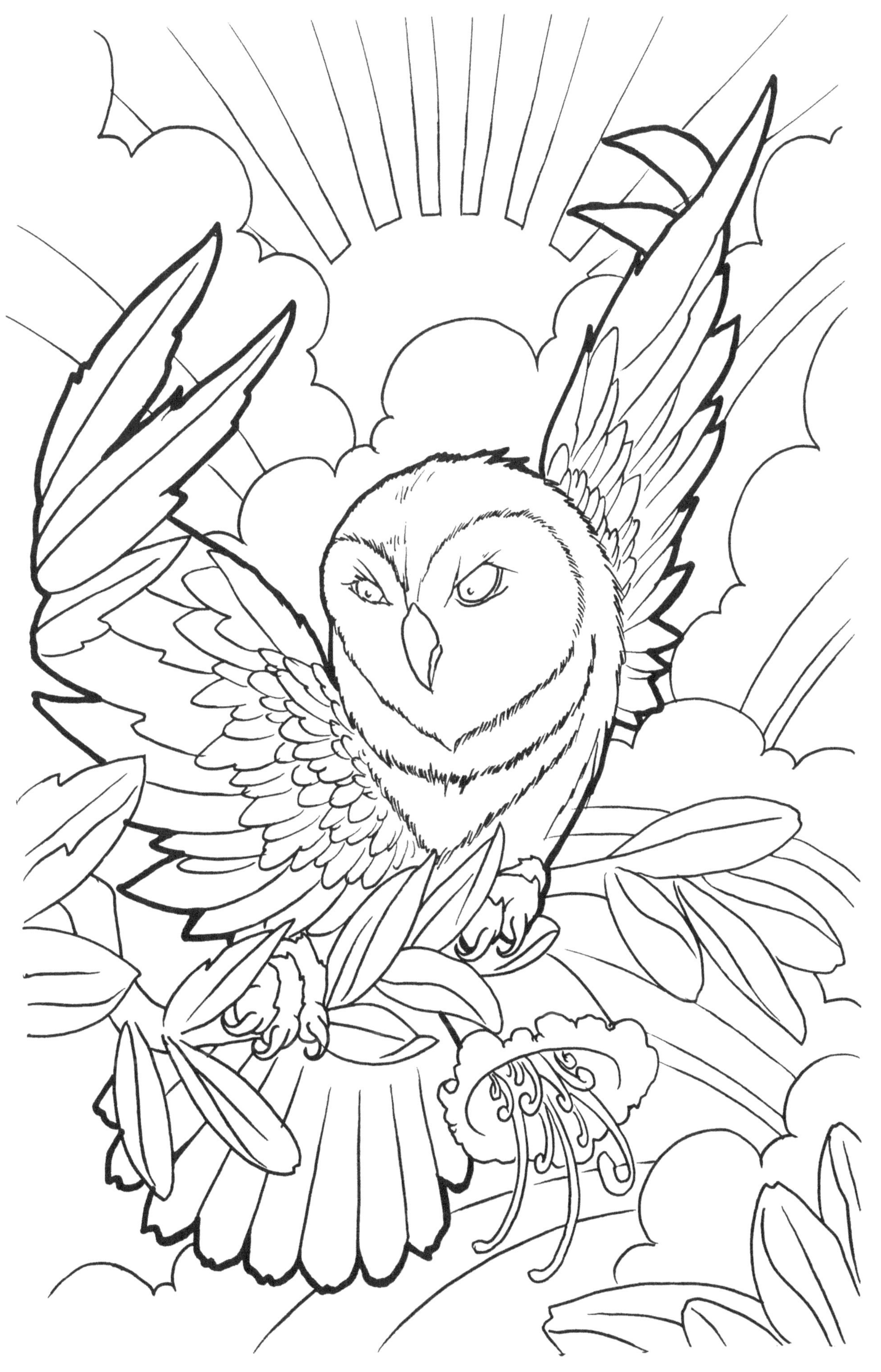

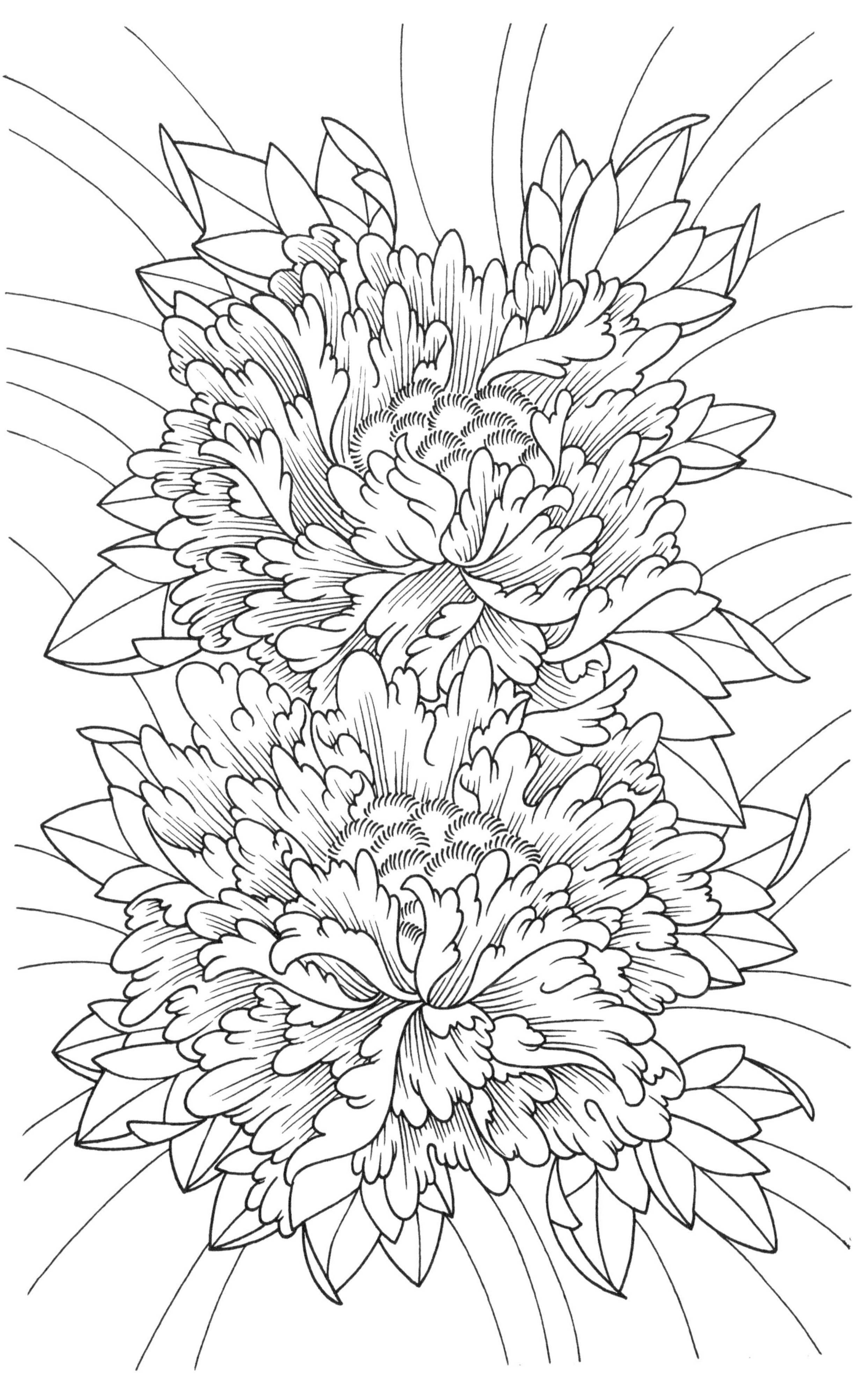

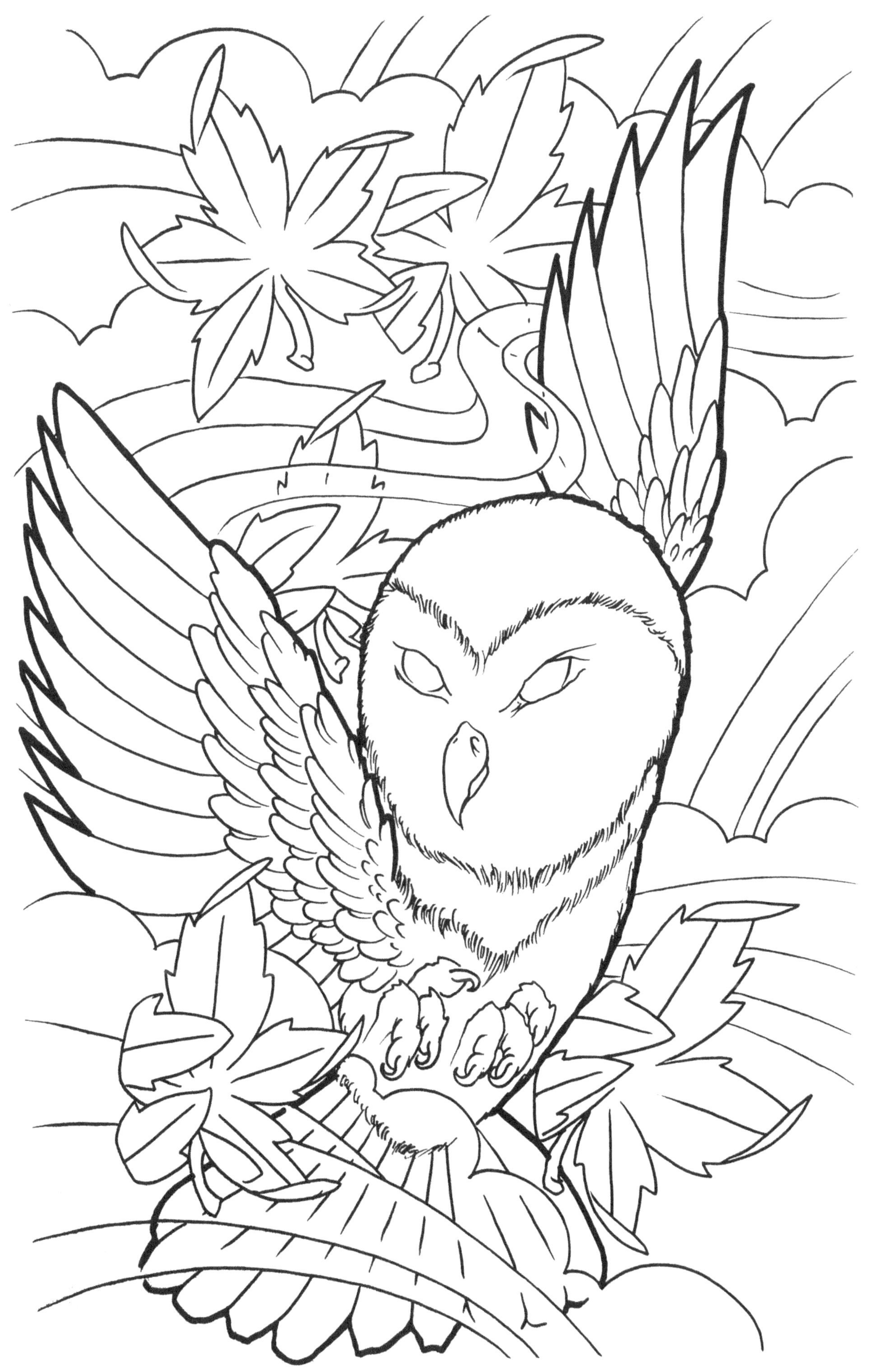

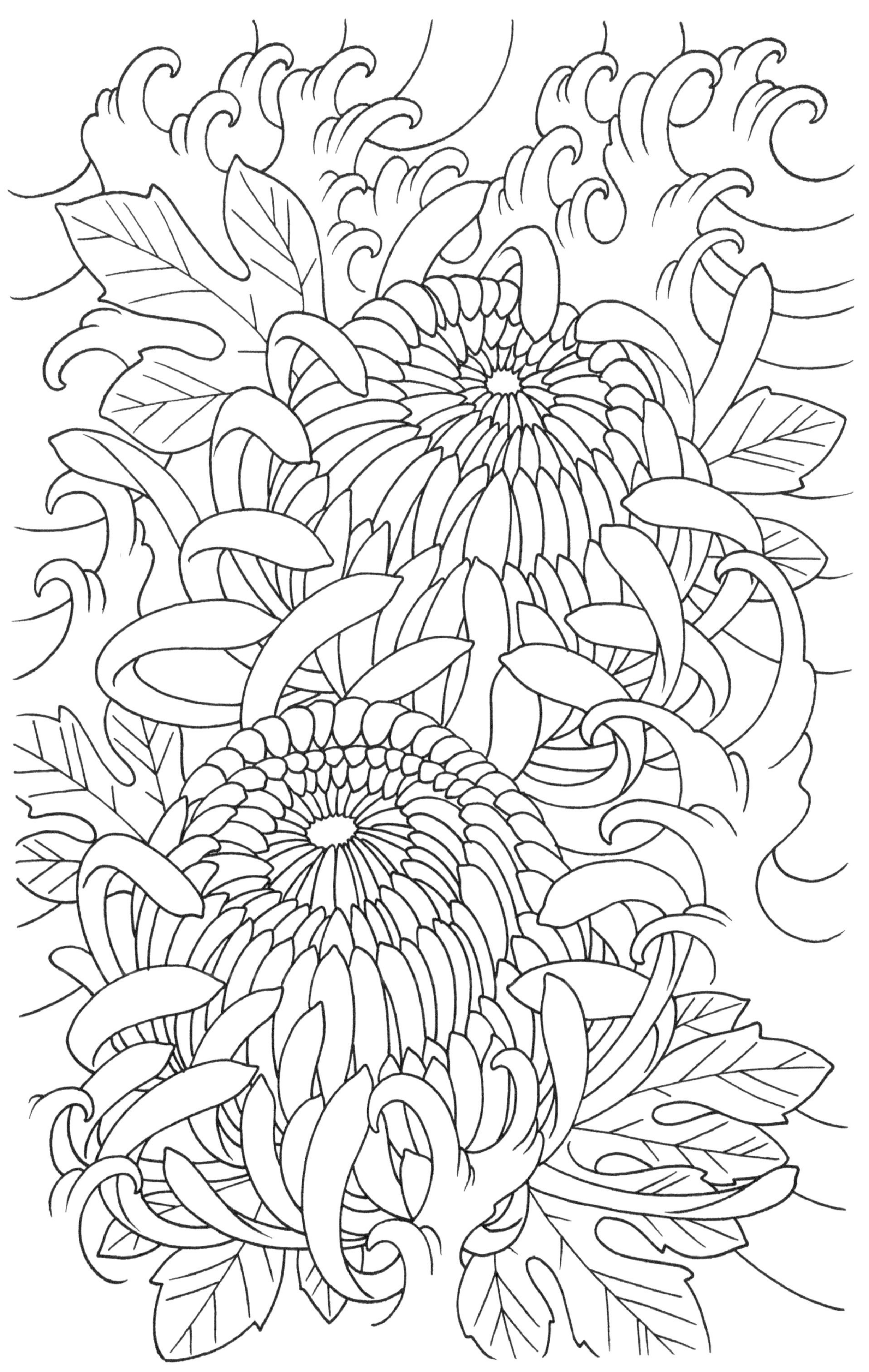

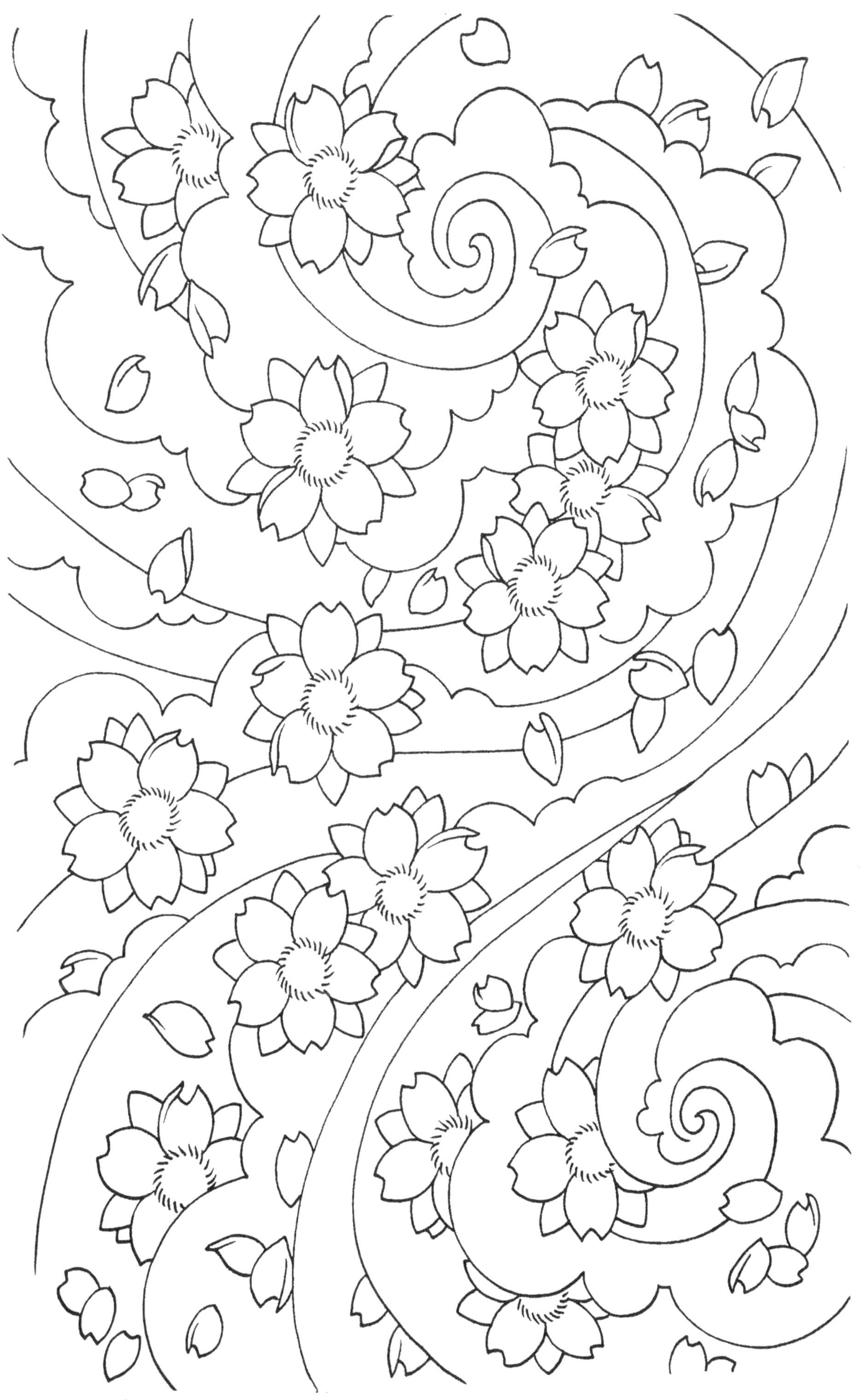

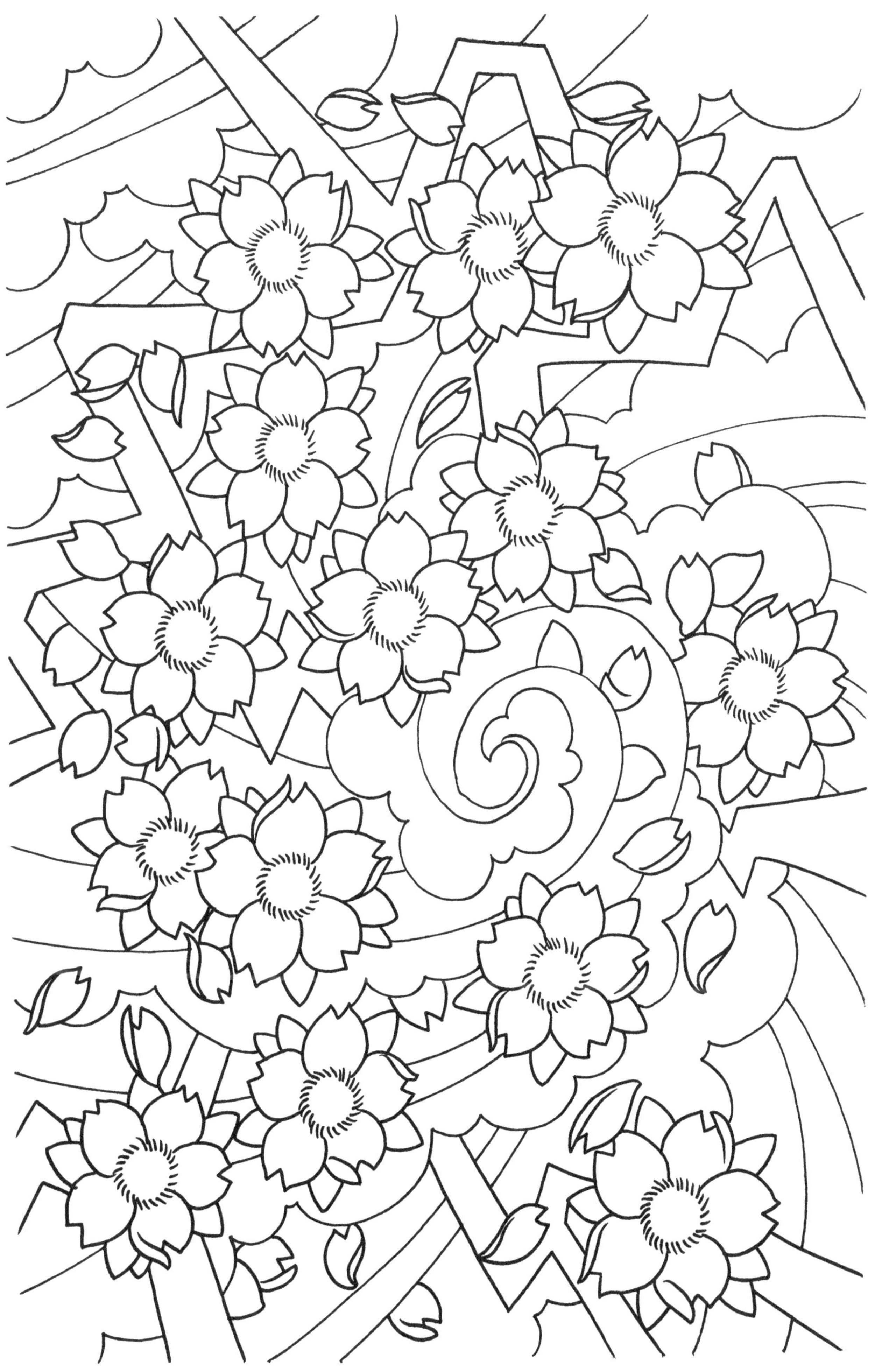

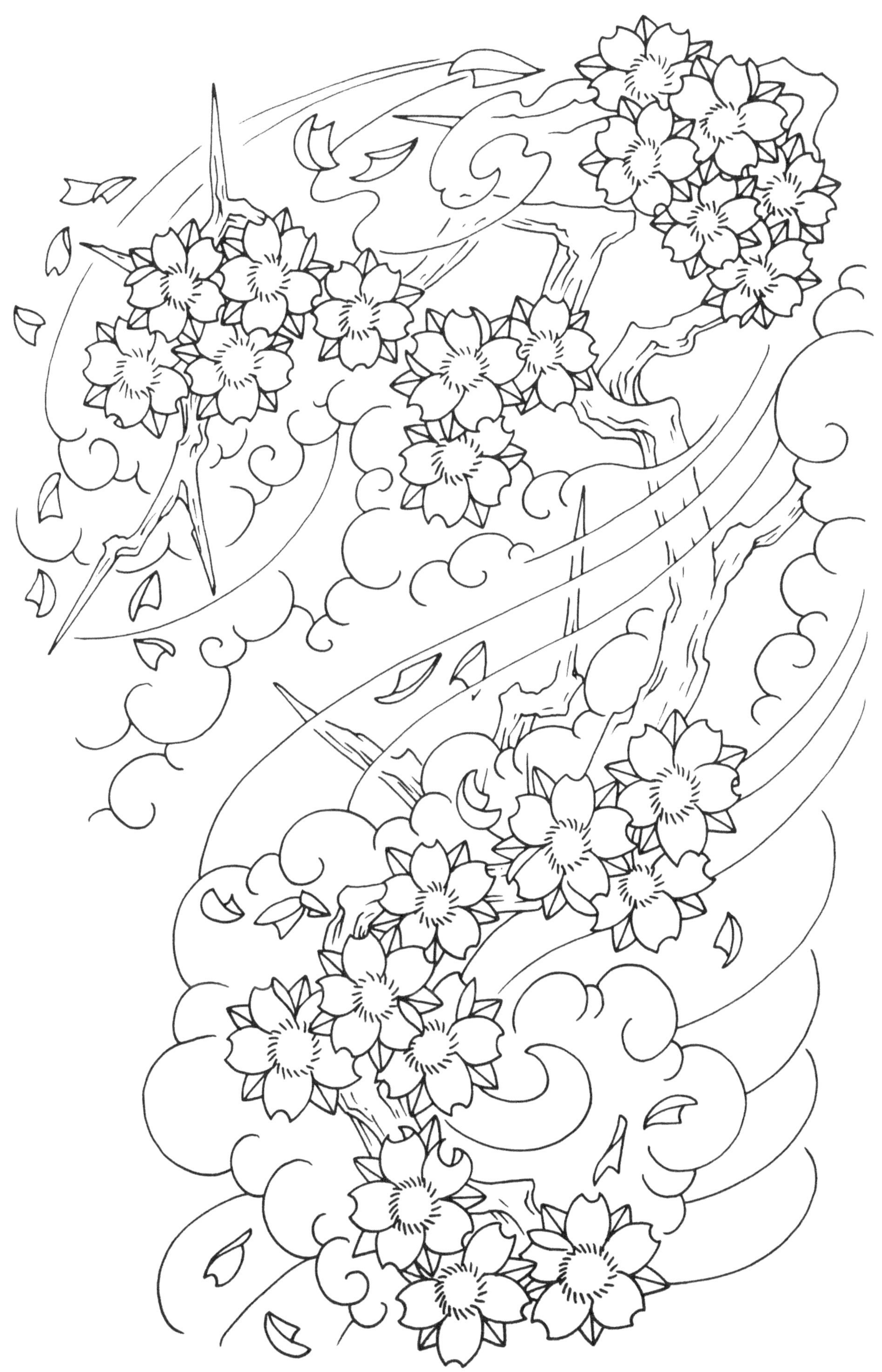

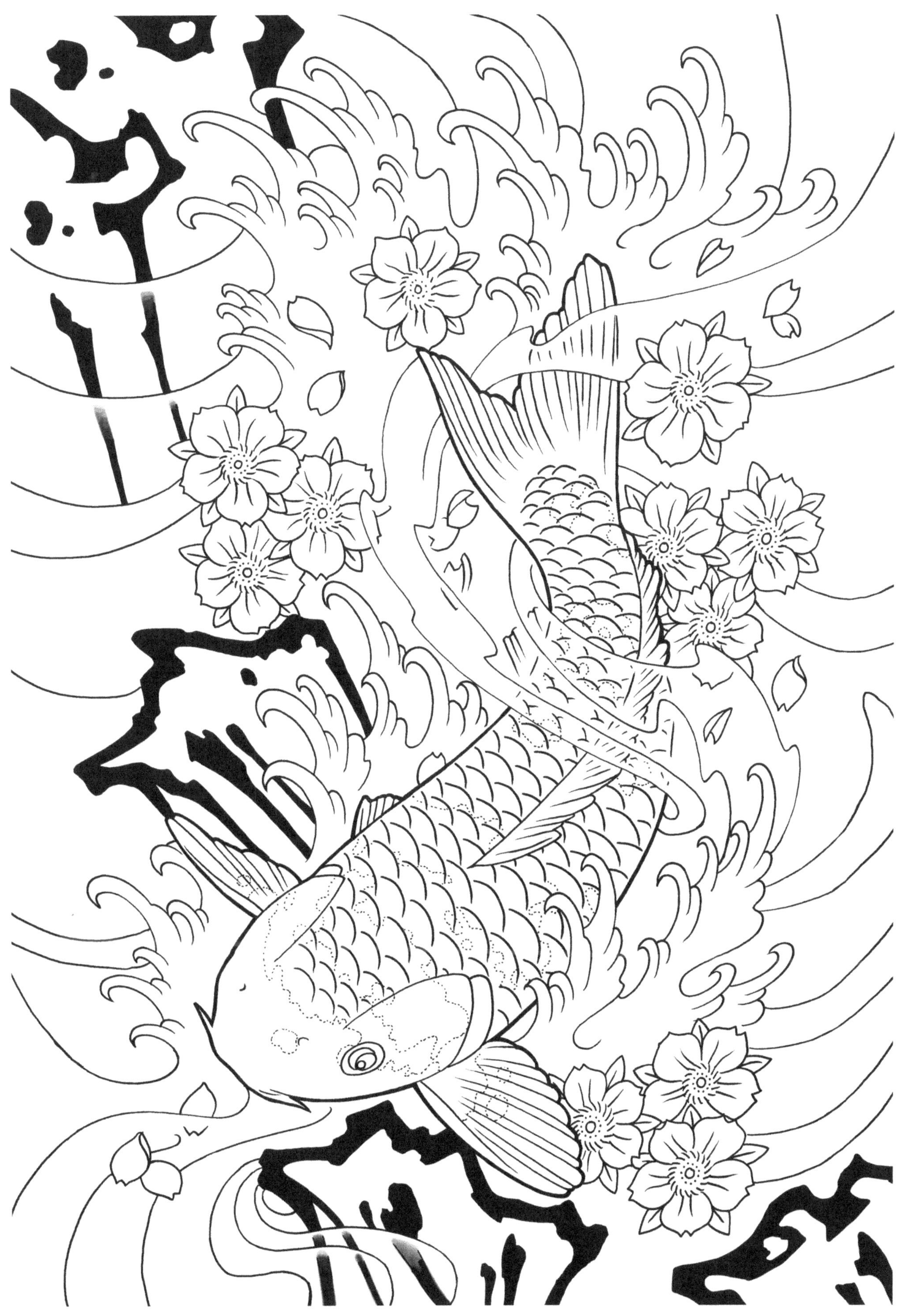

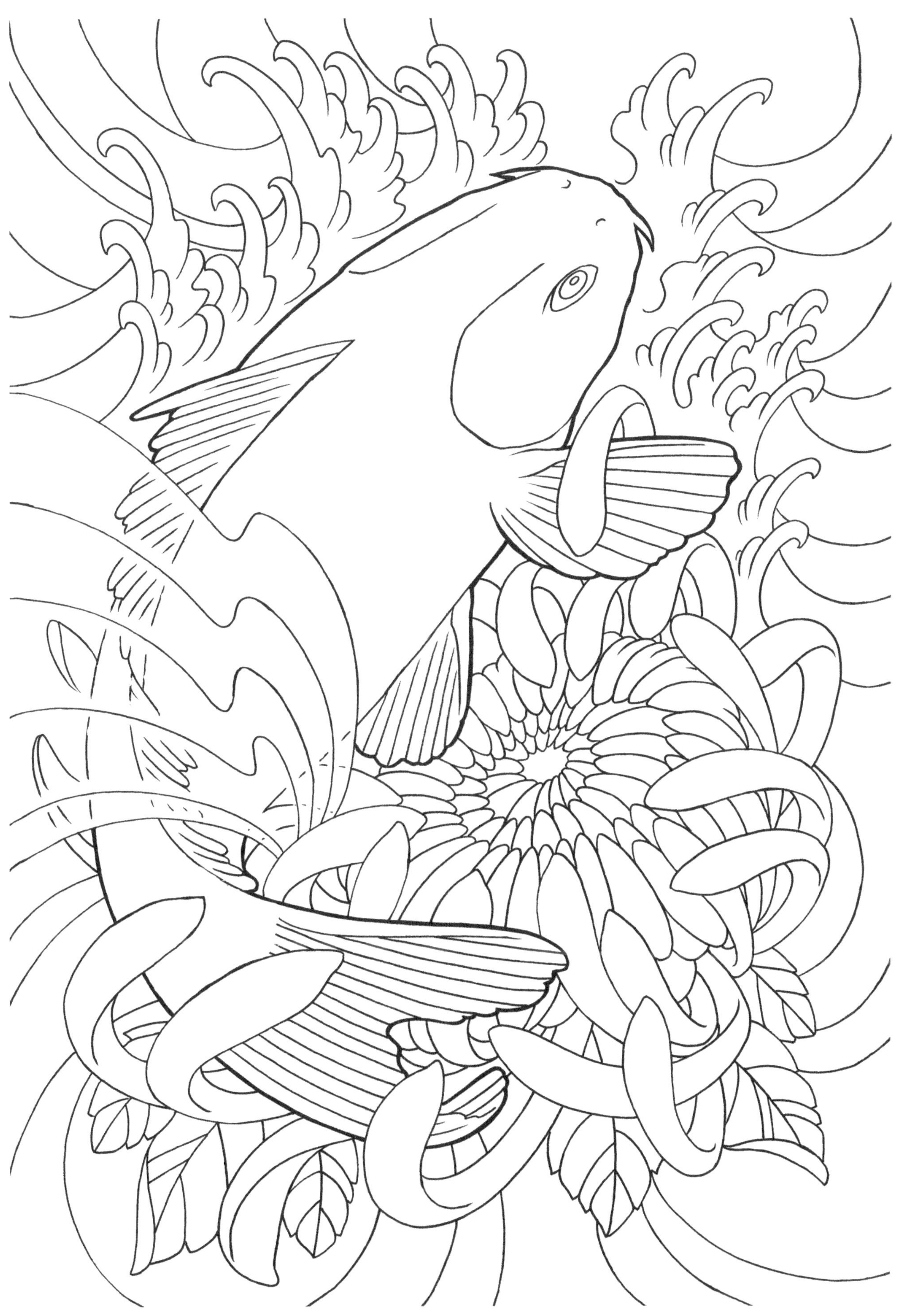

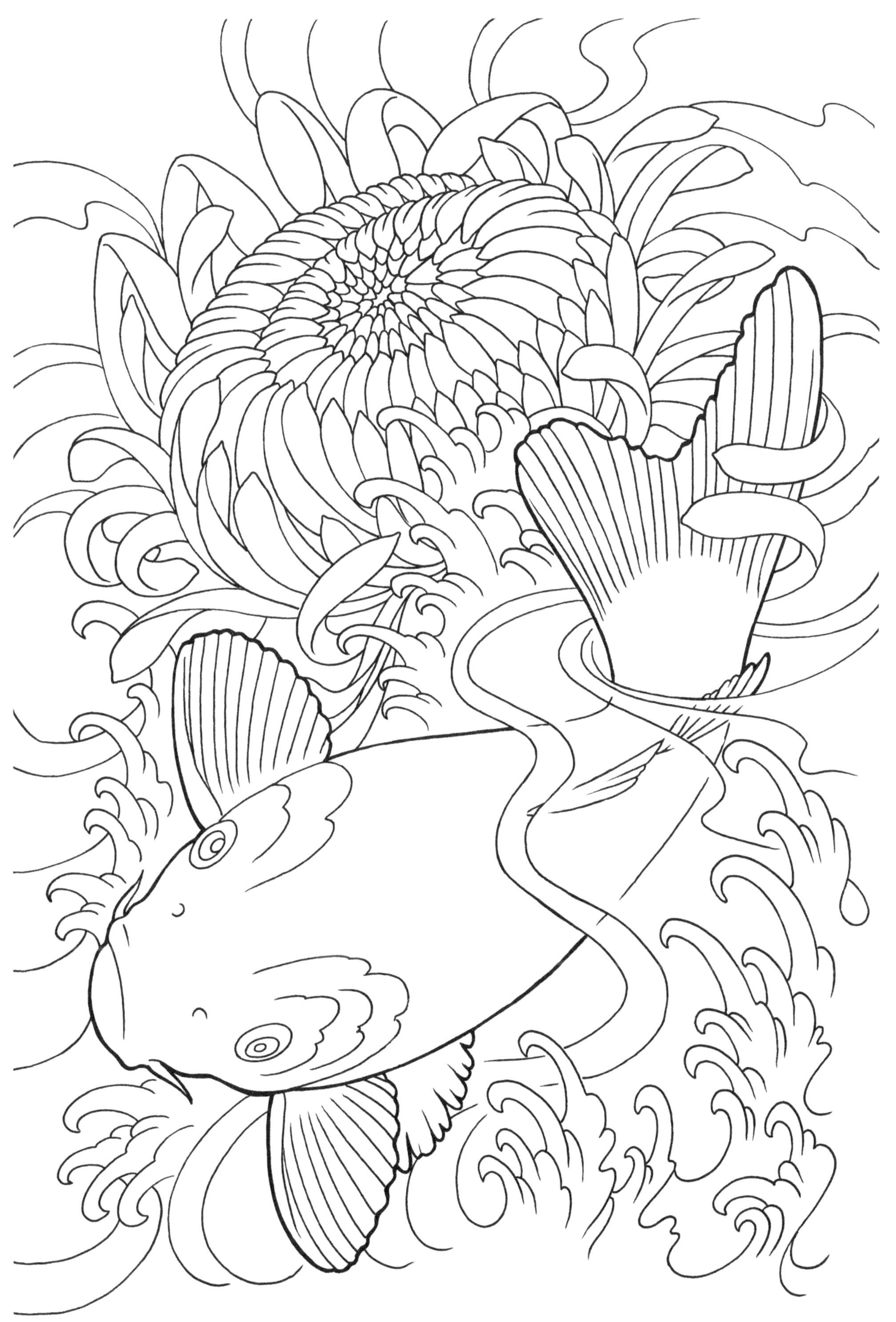

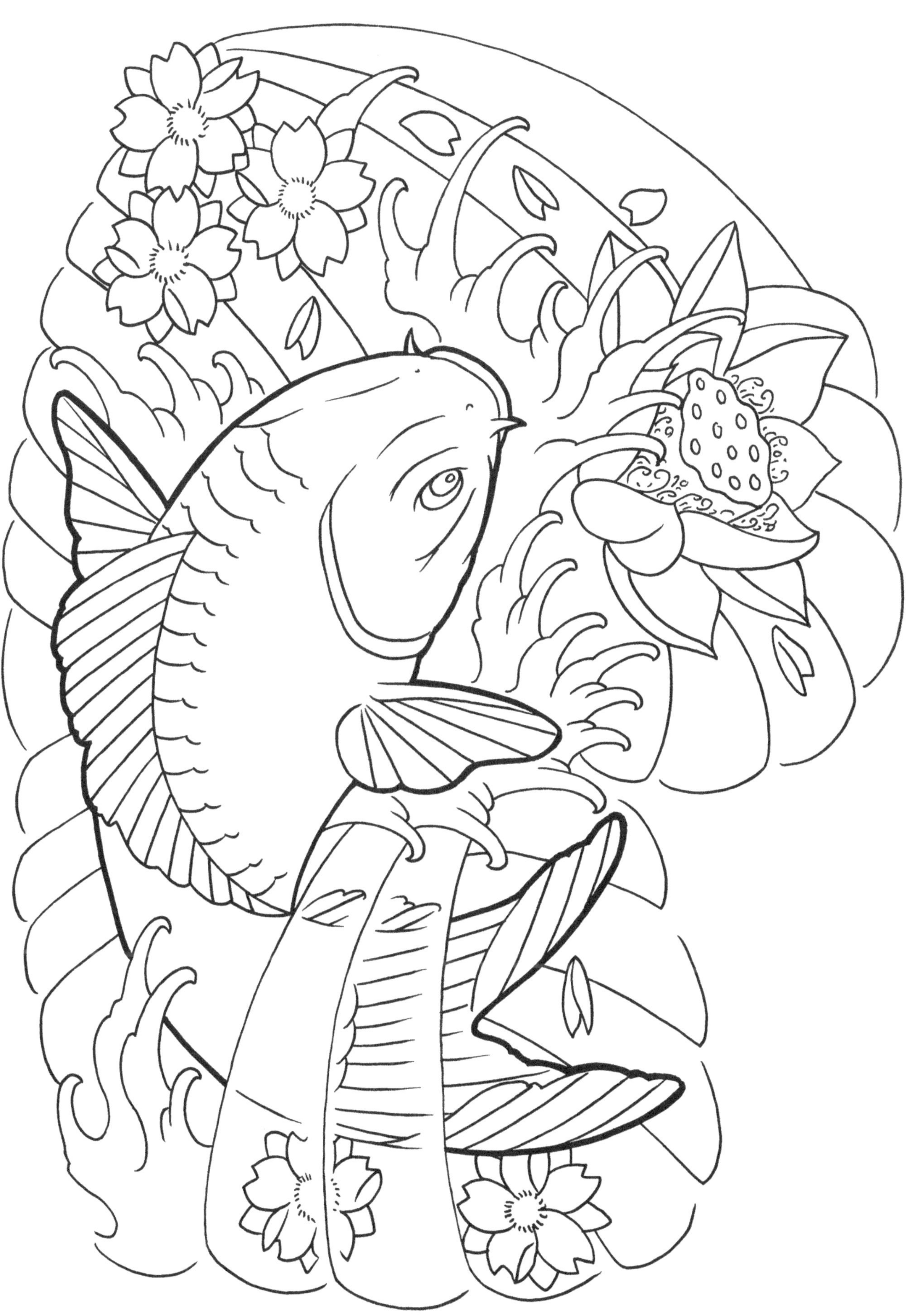

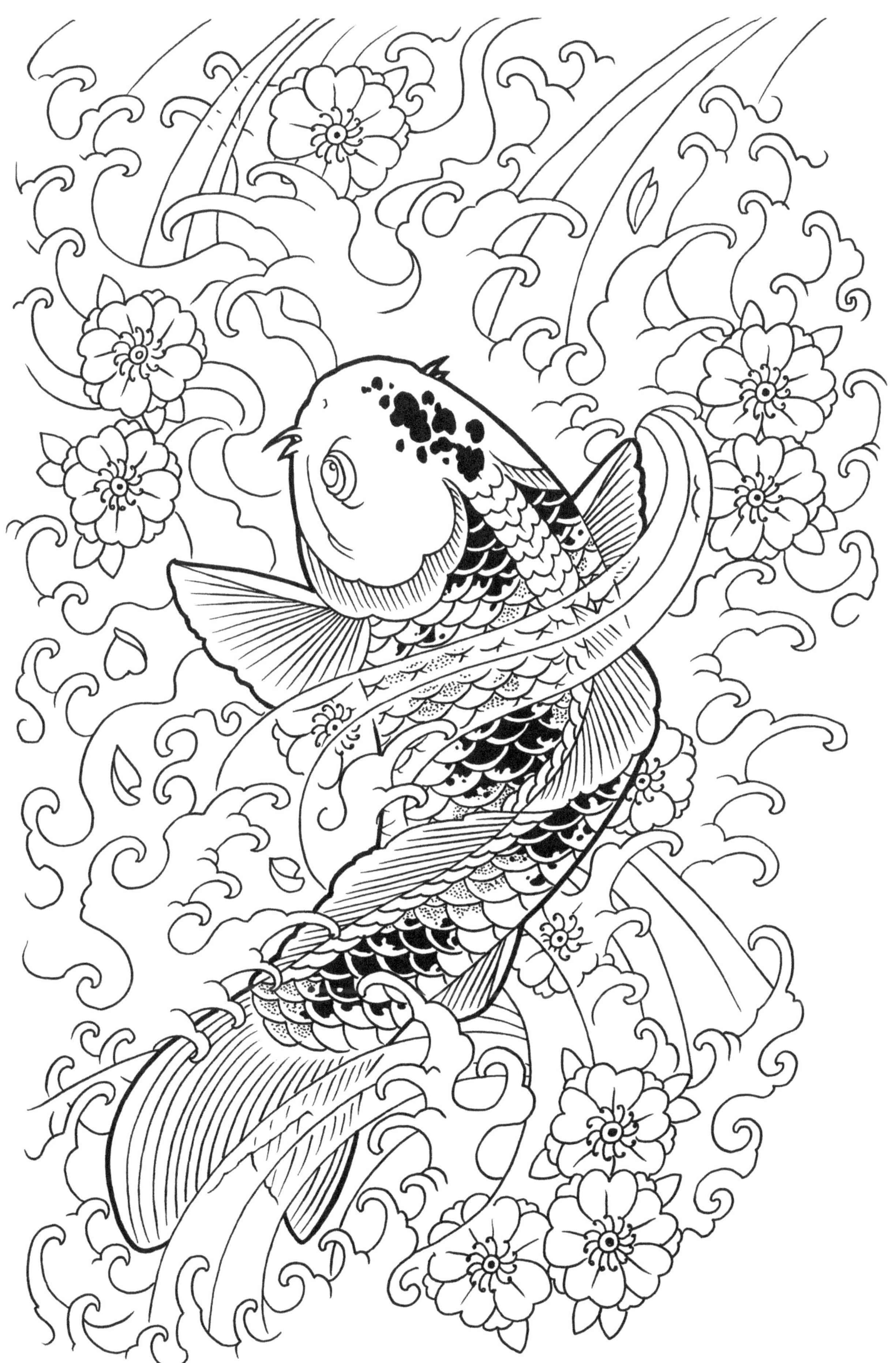

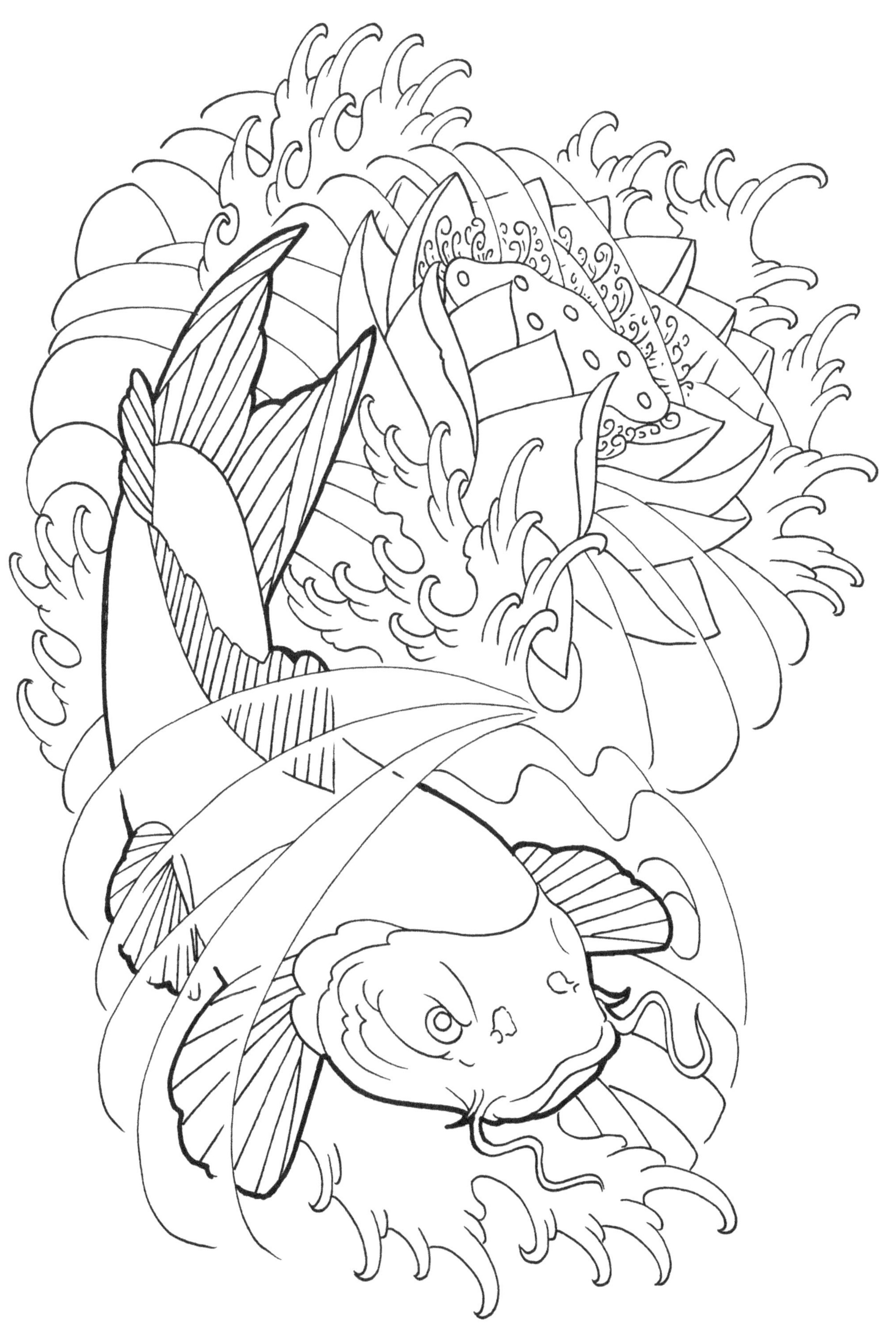

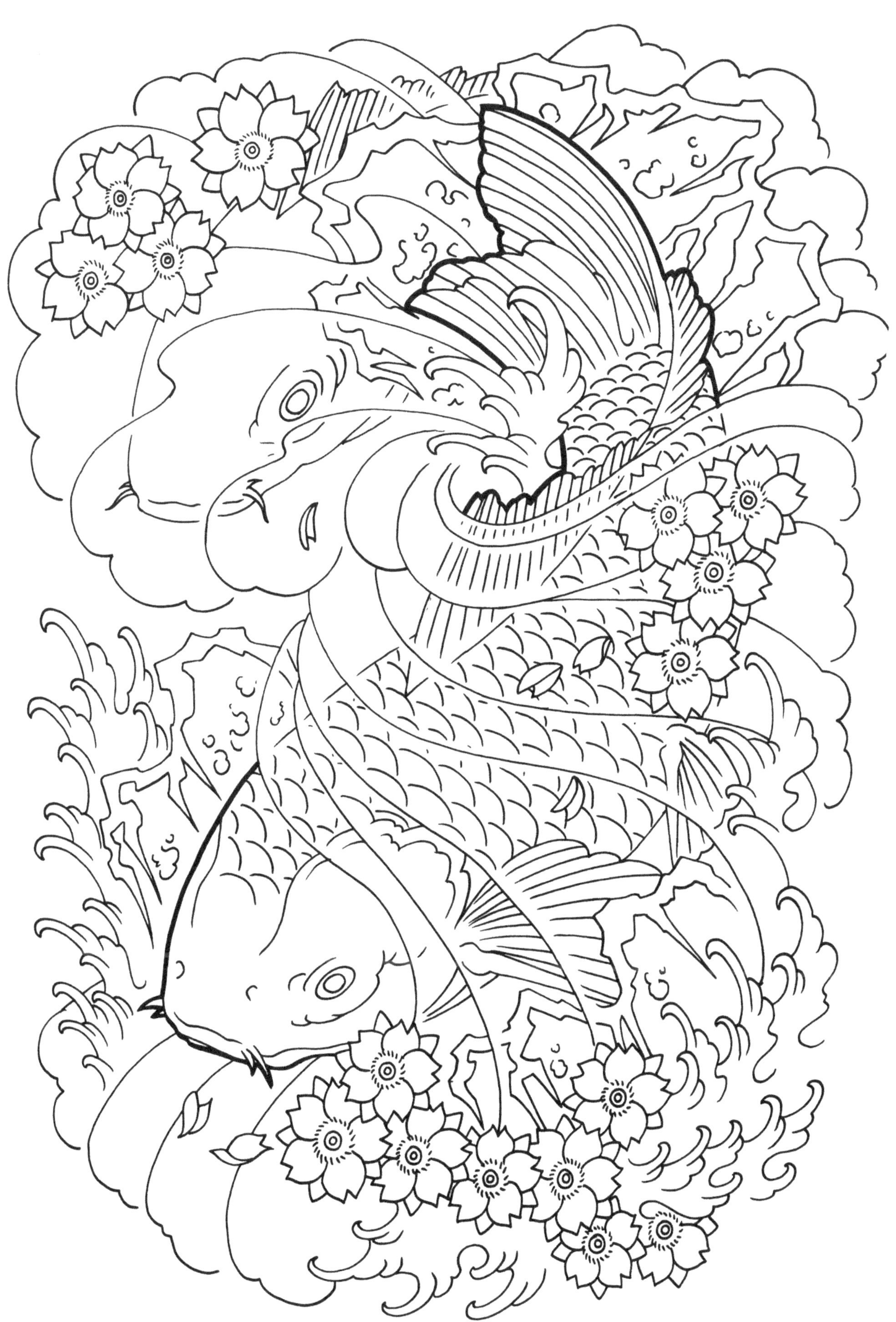

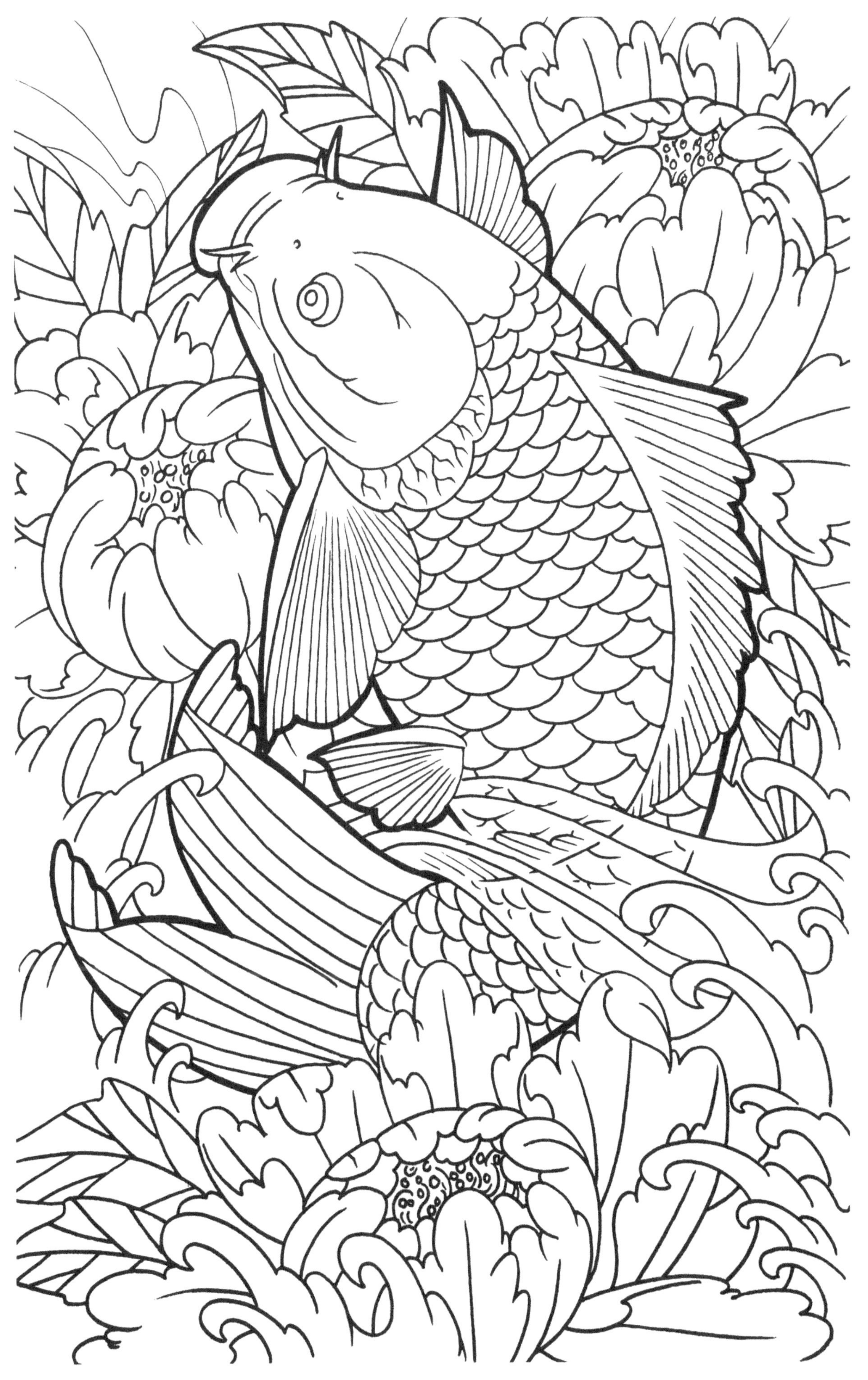

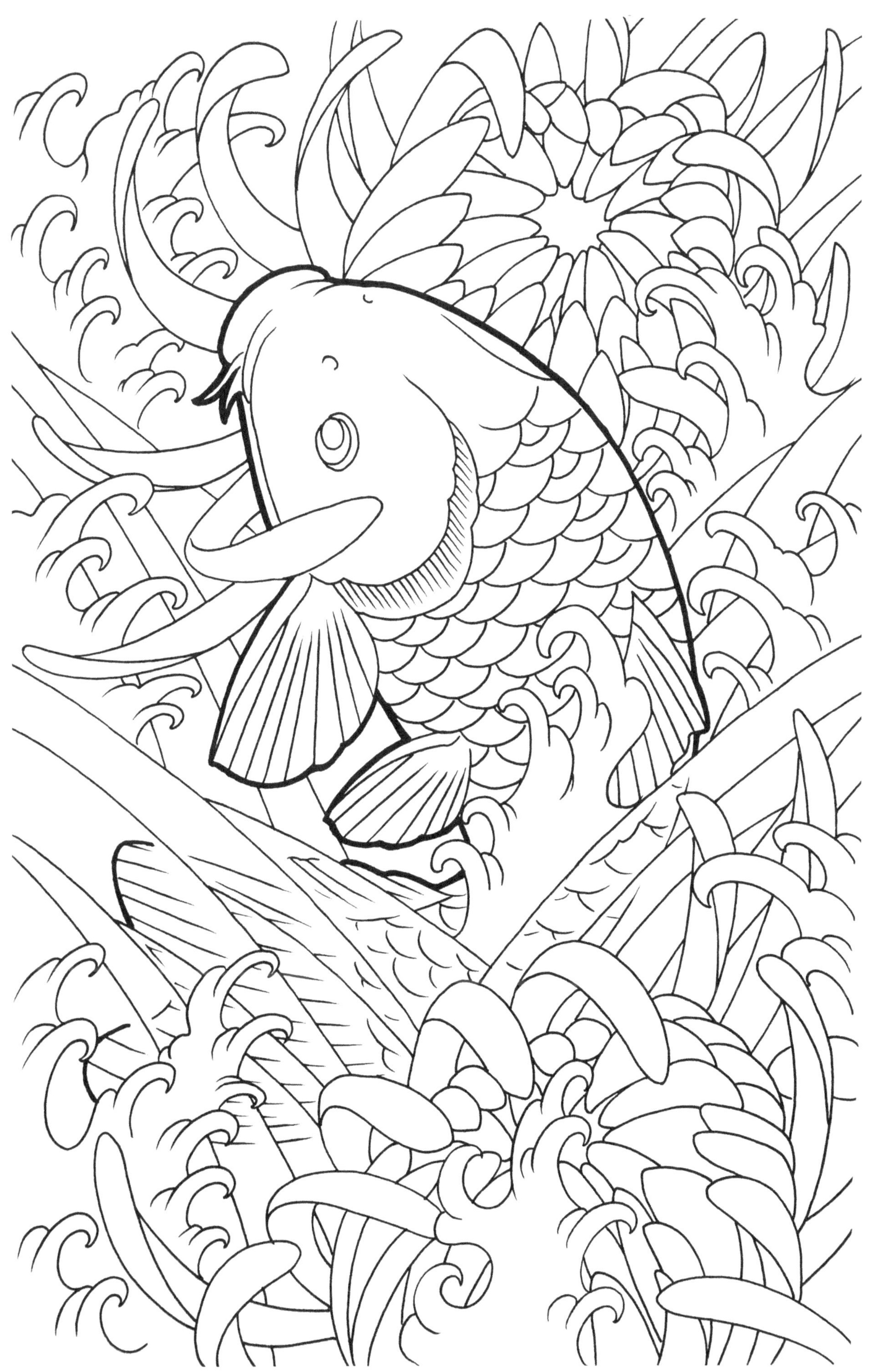

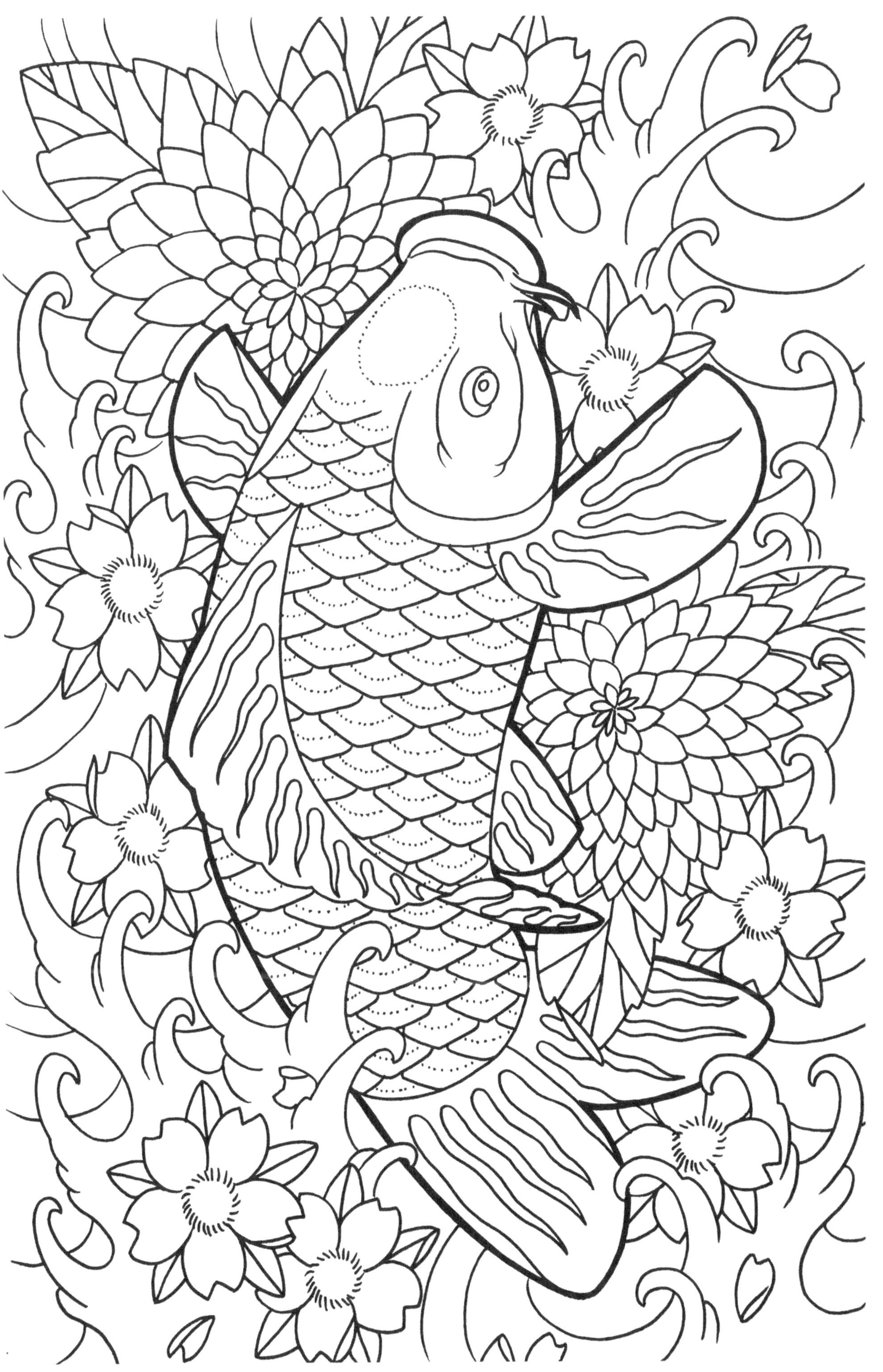

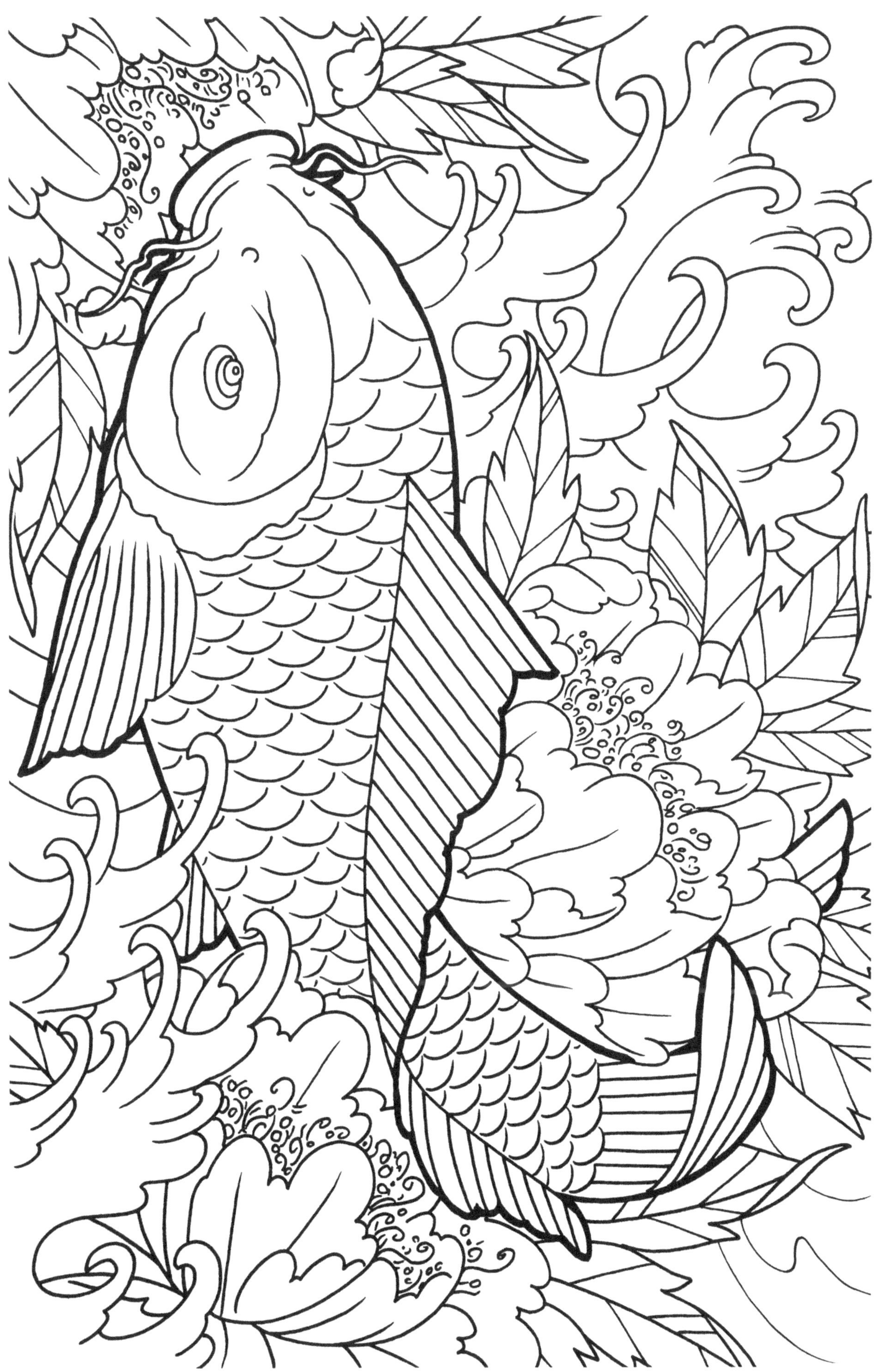

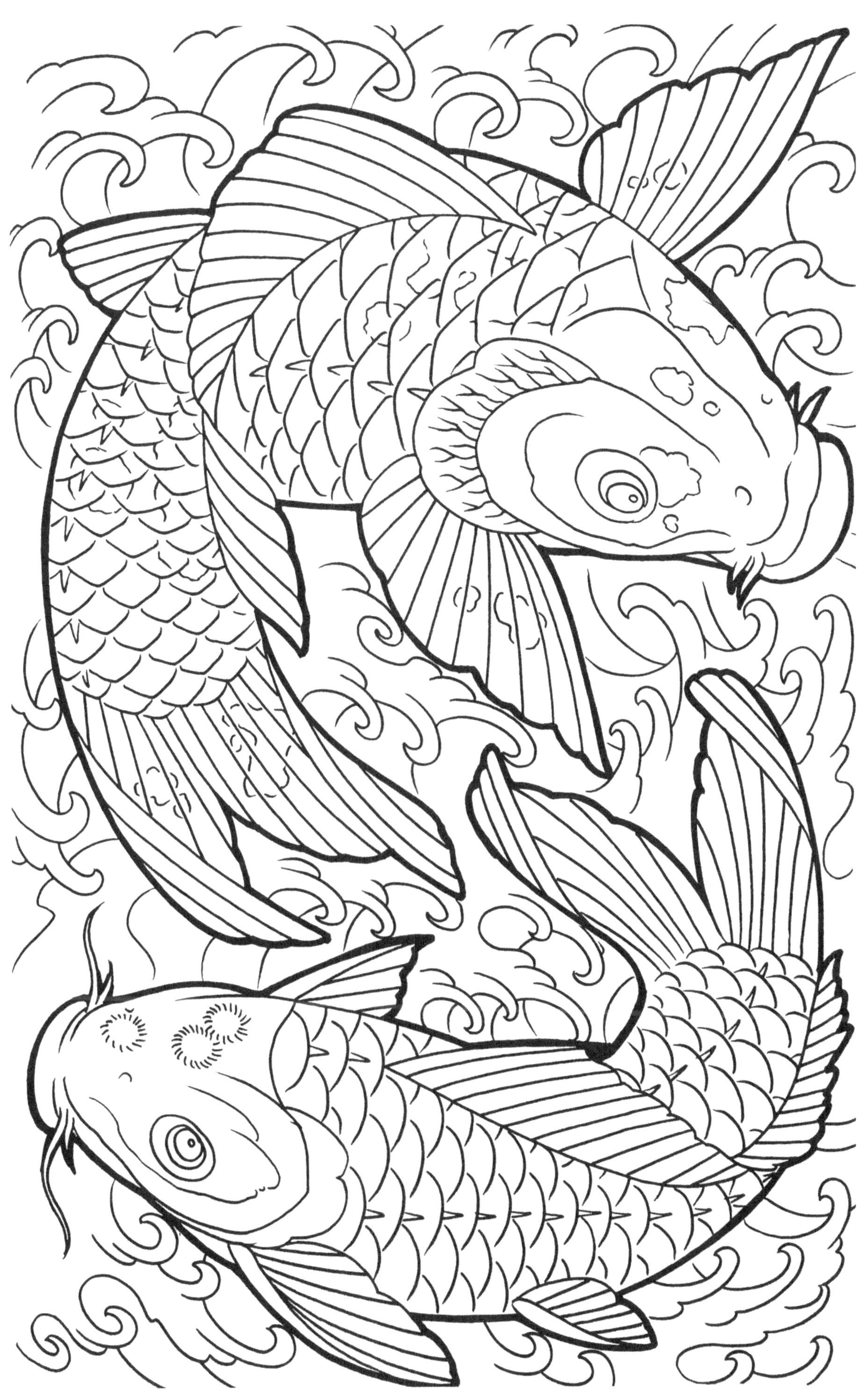

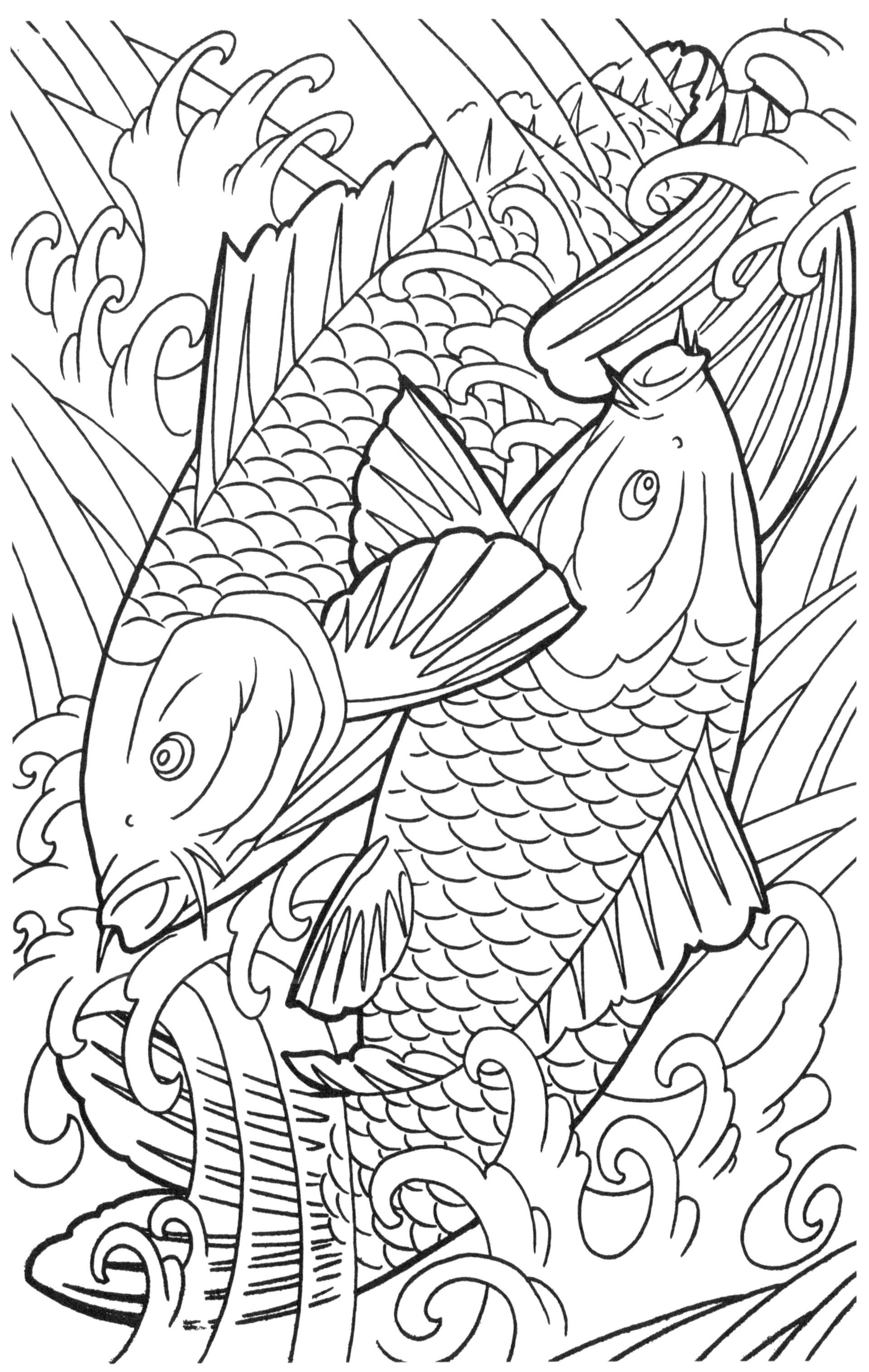

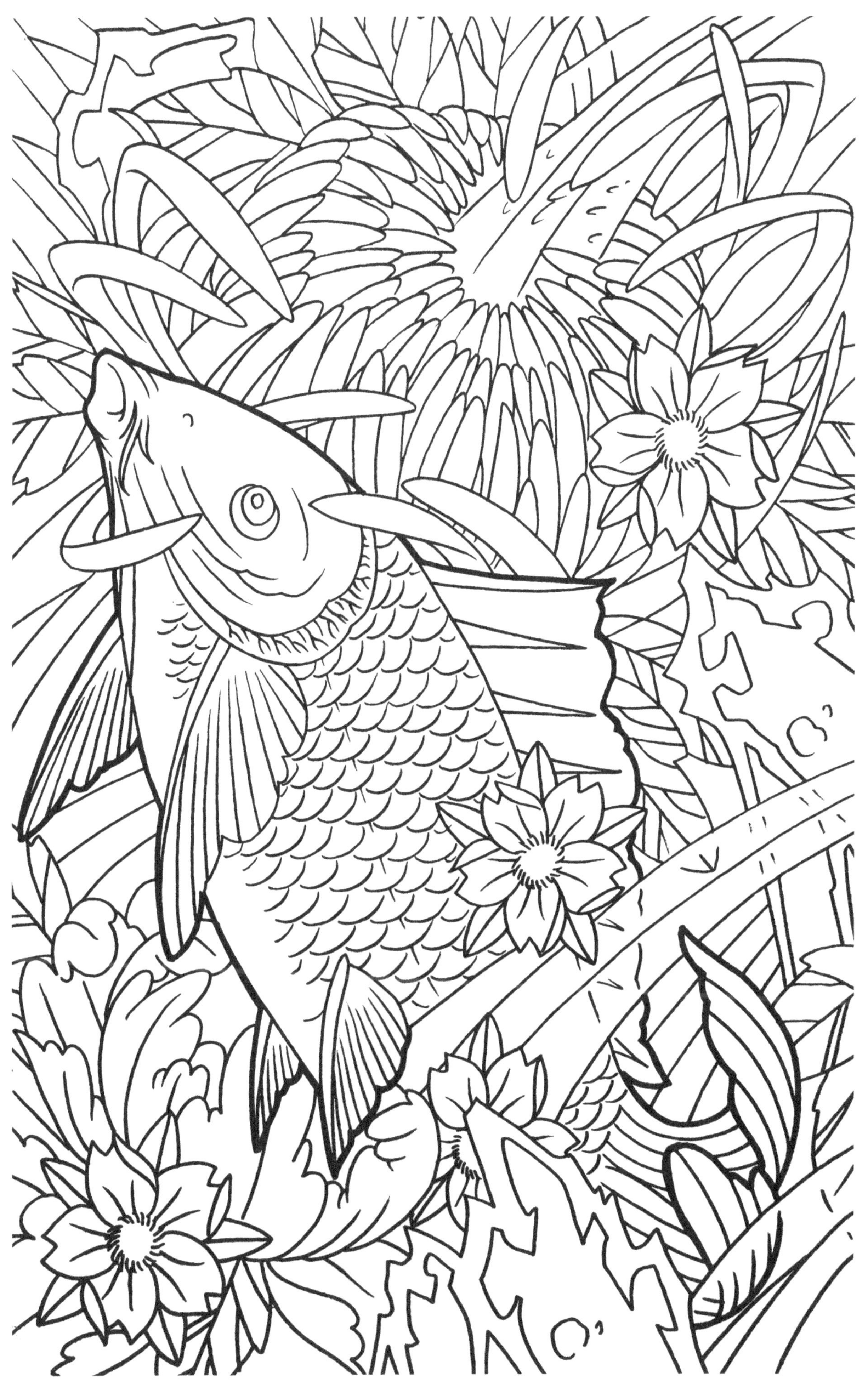

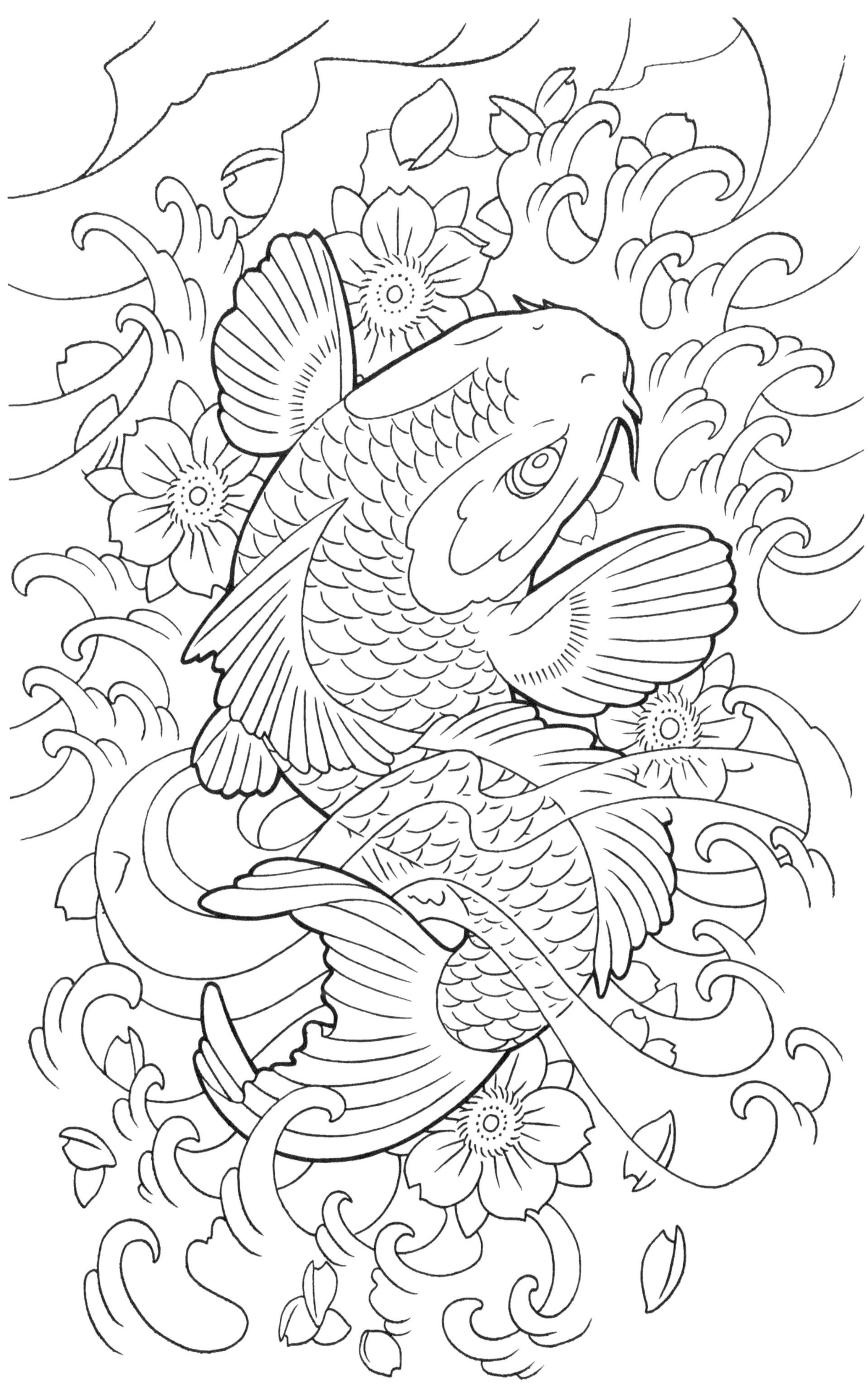

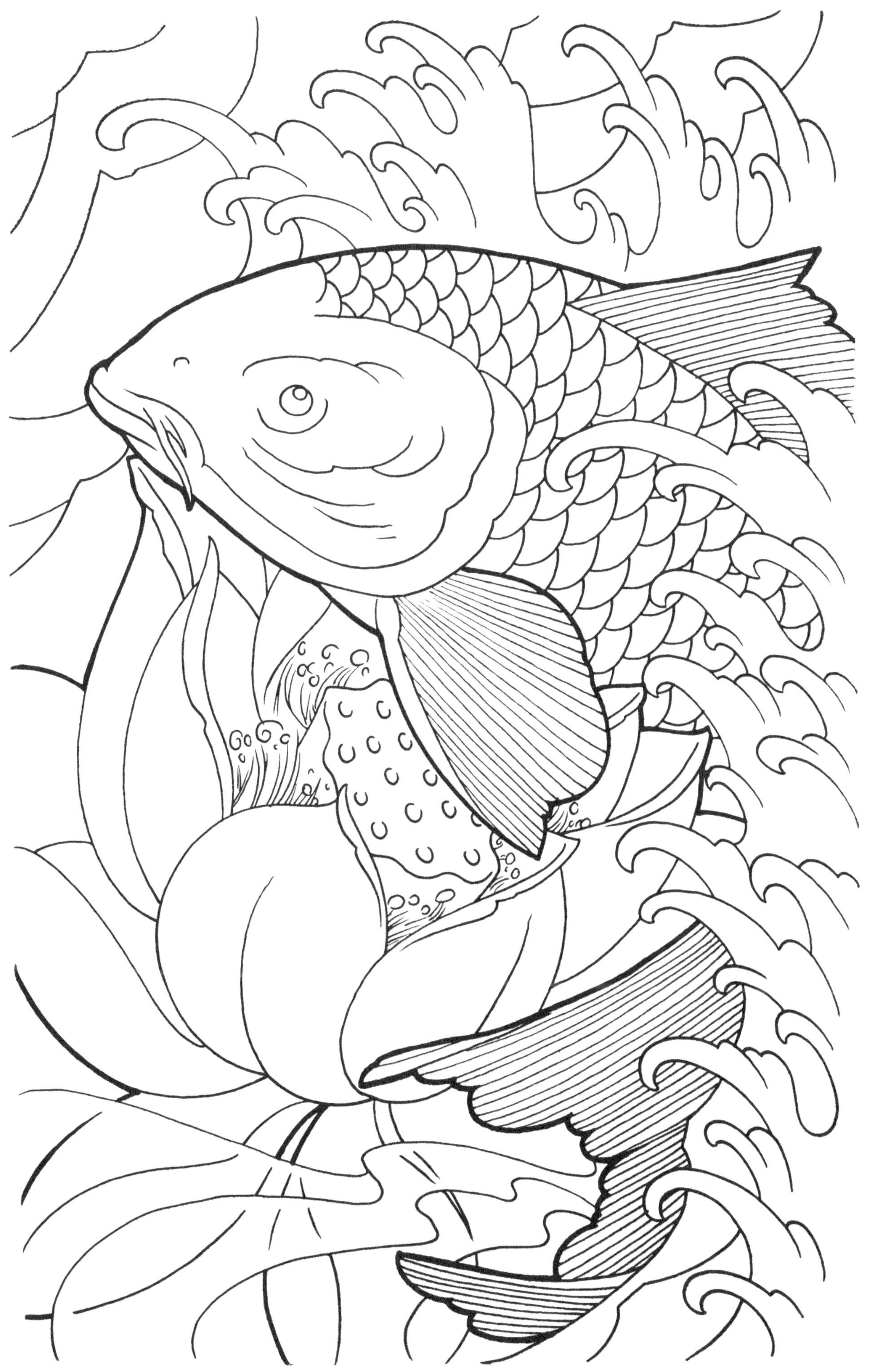

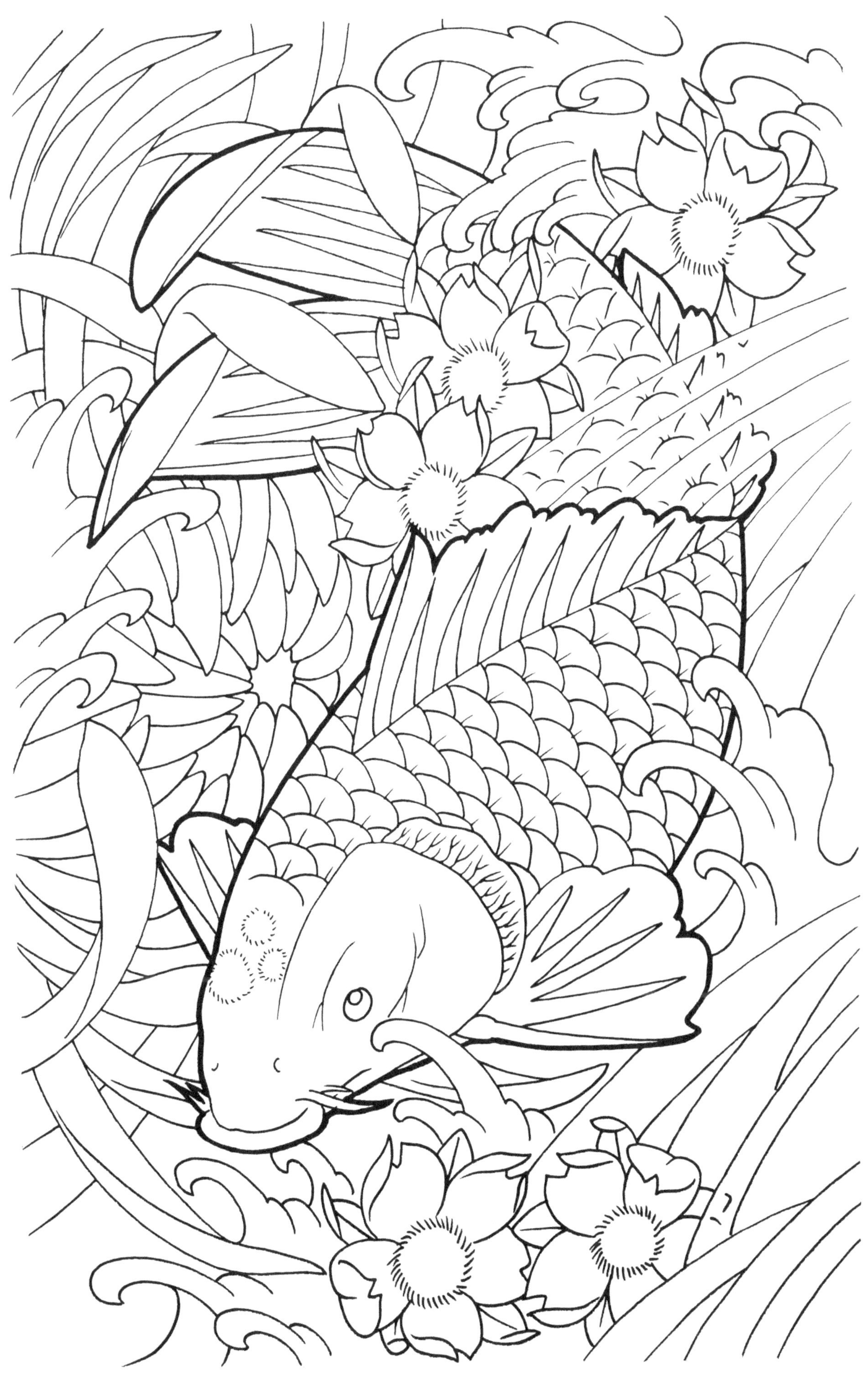

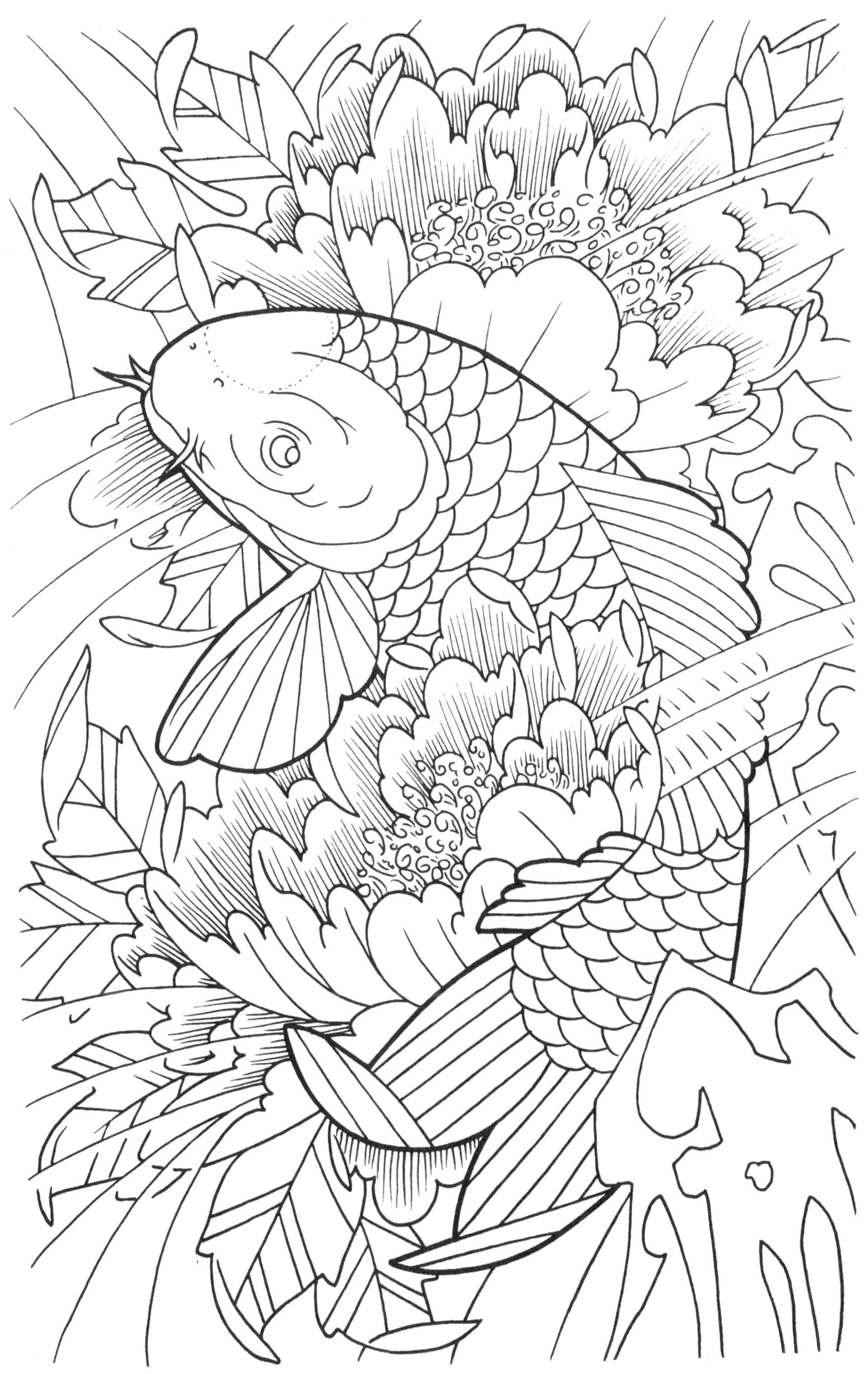

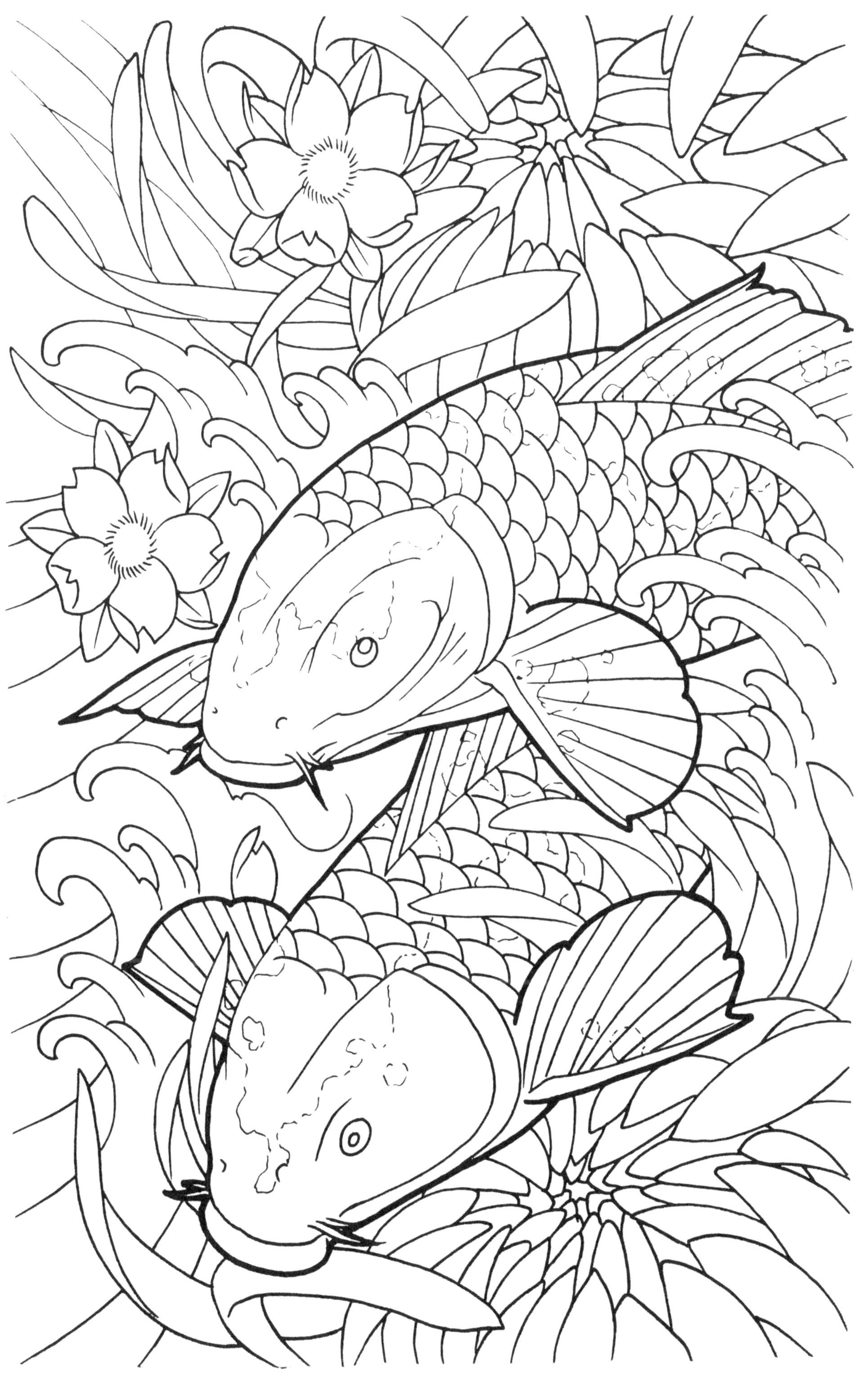

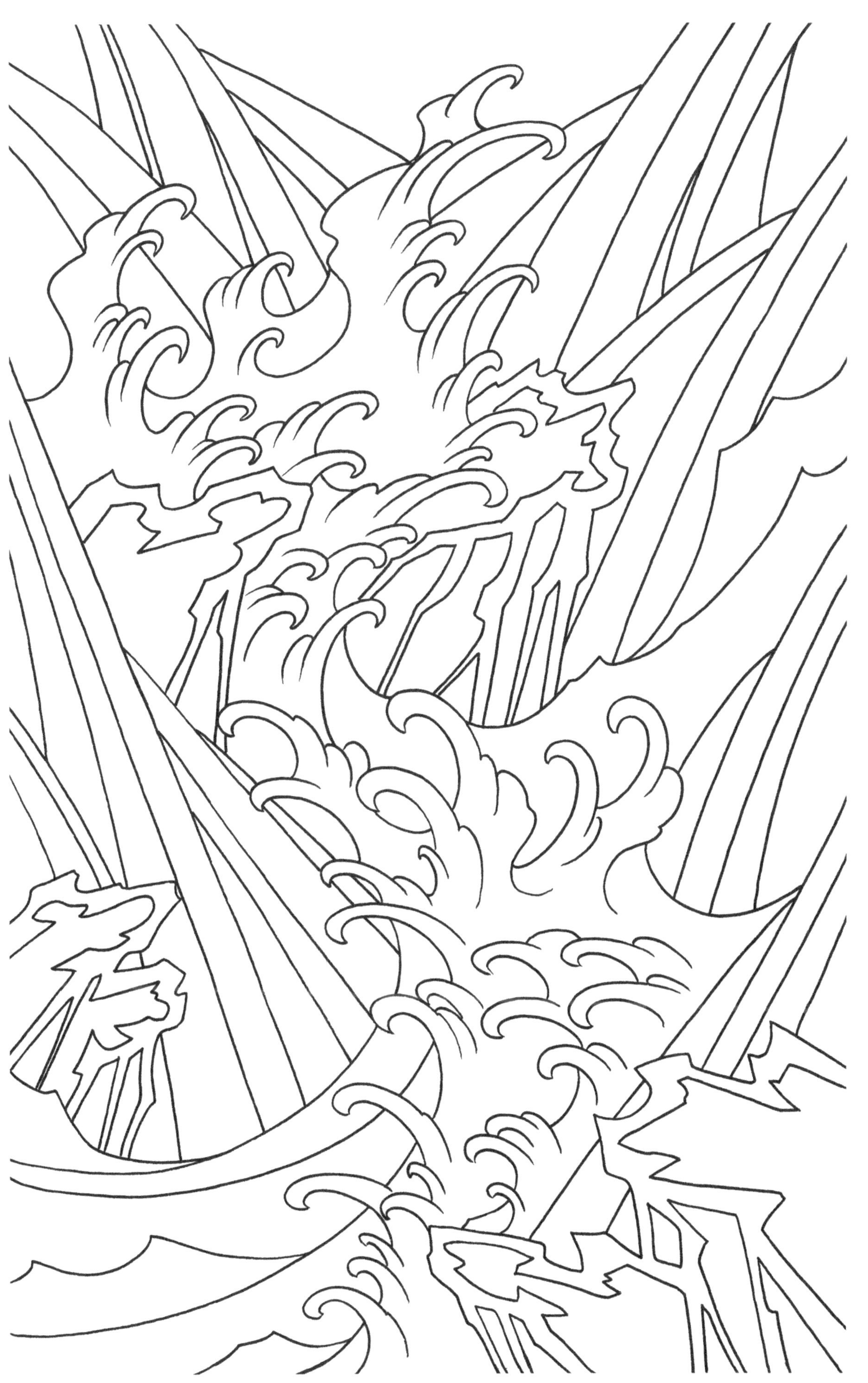

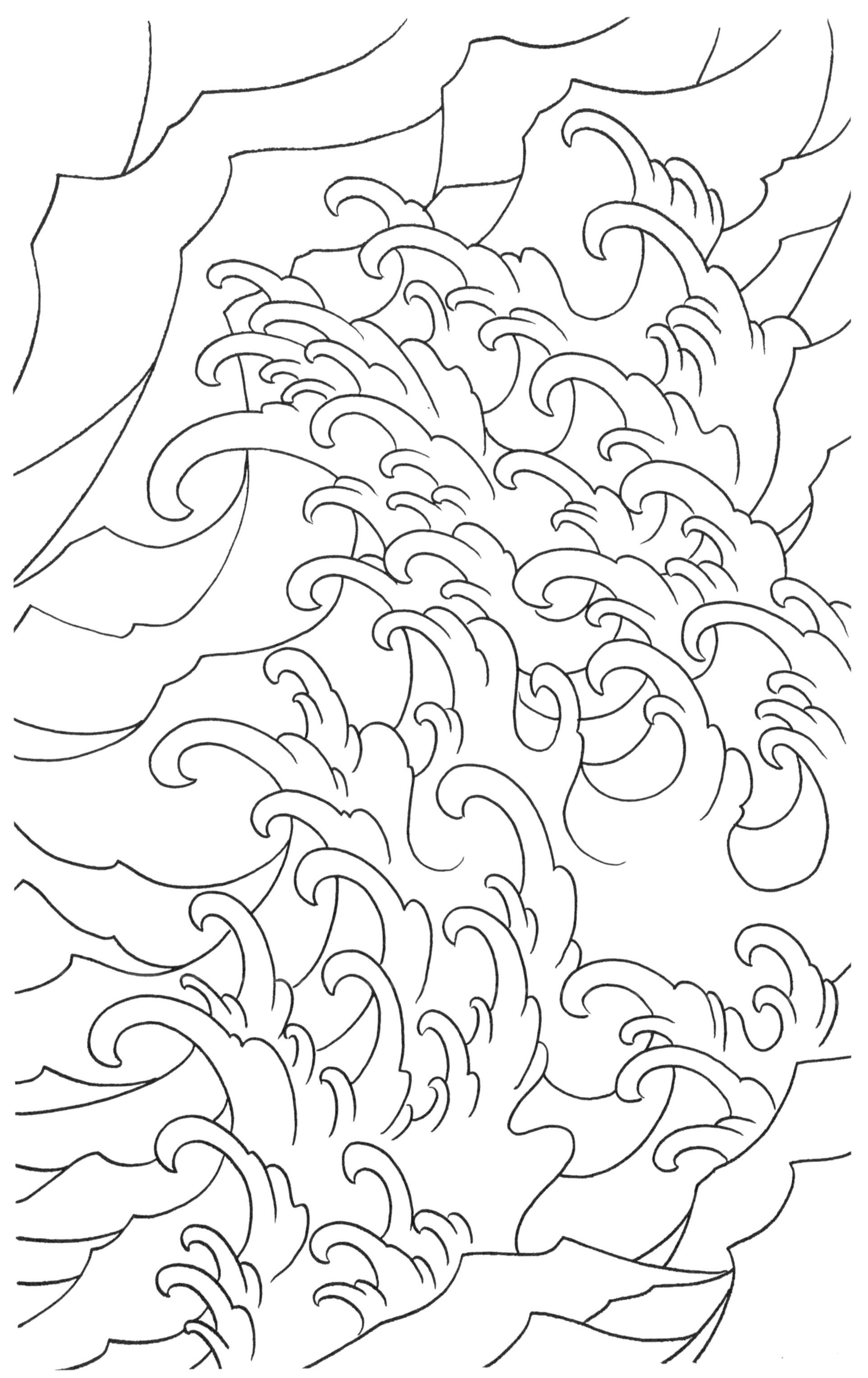

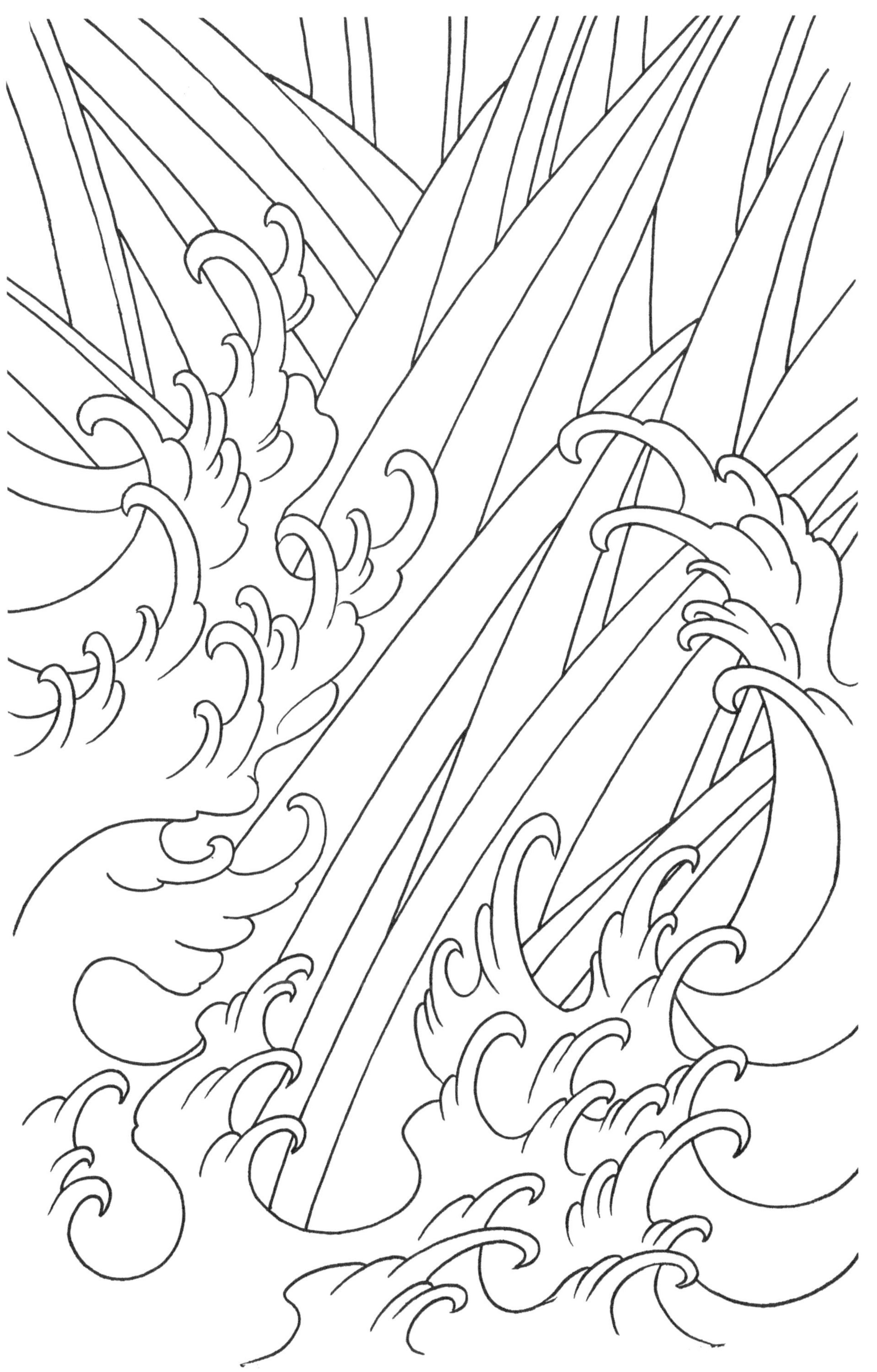

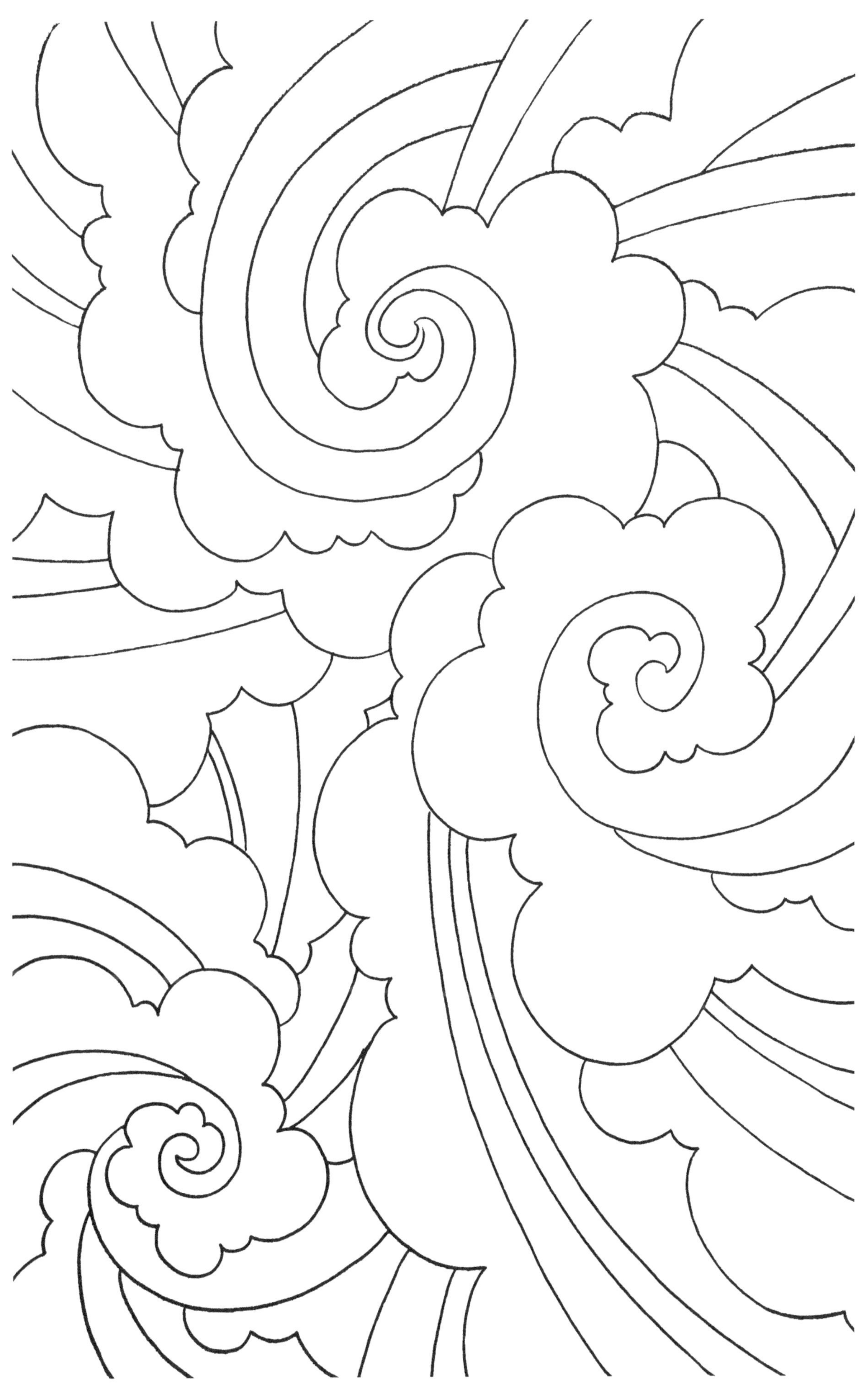

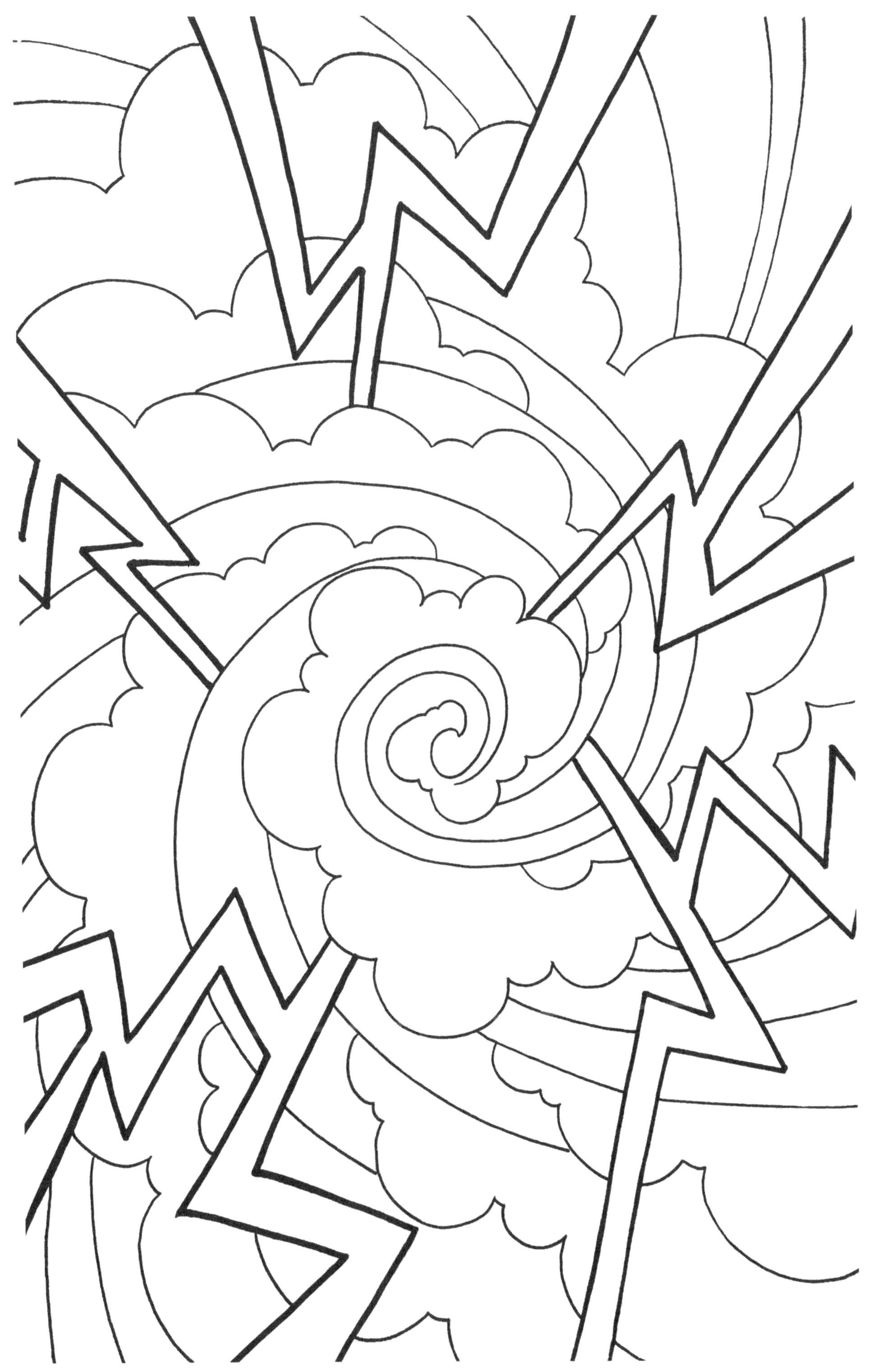

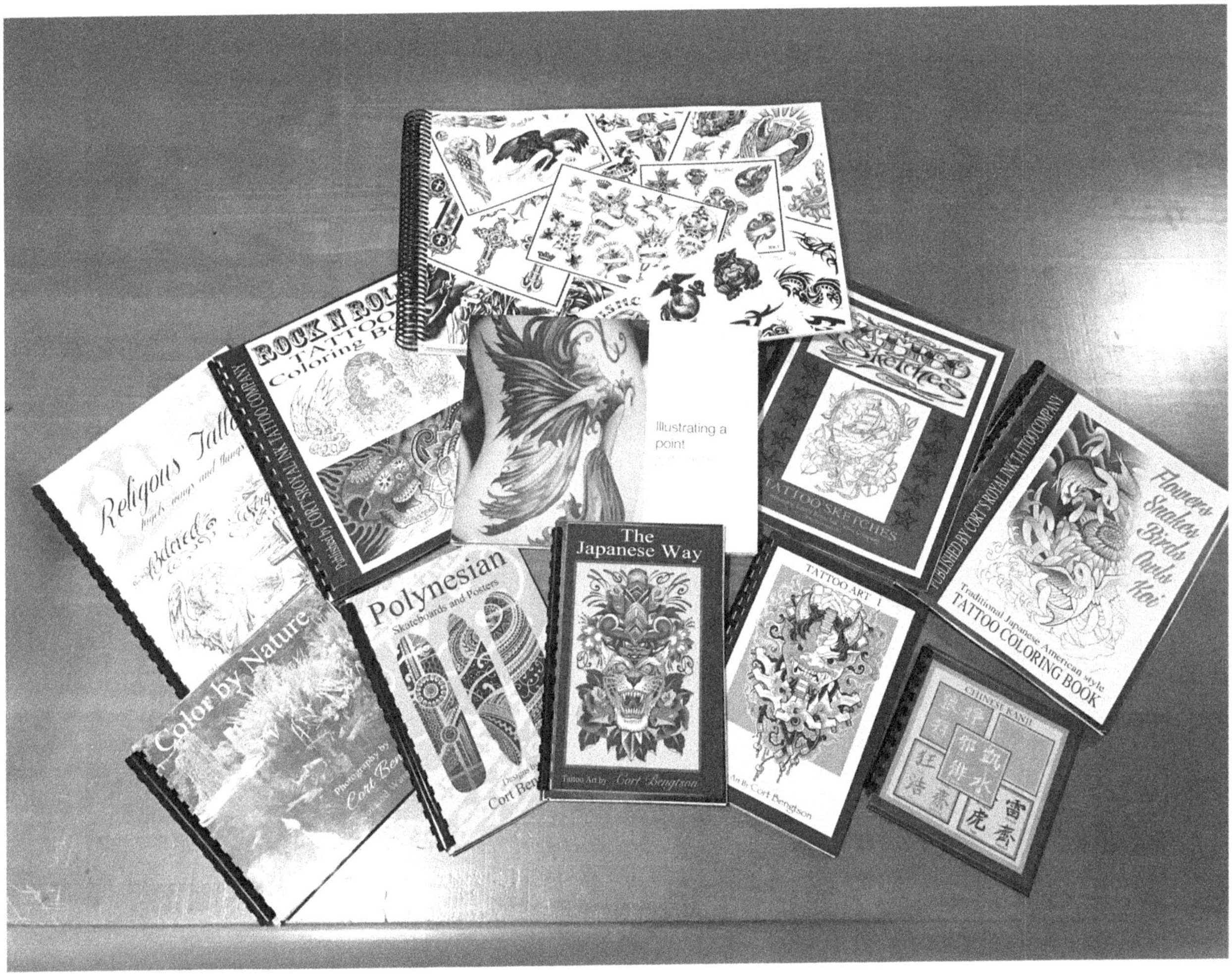

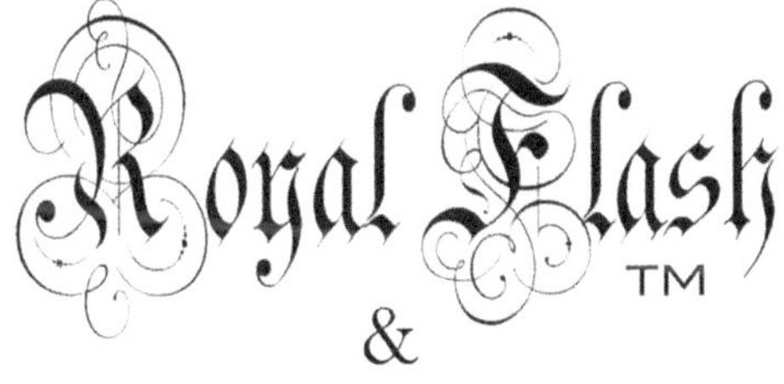

Check out these other great books,
Flash, Prints and original Art from

Royal Flash ™

&

Cort's Royal Ink Tattoo Company

@ royalink.631 on ebay

Contact us @ cortsroyalink@aol.com

See whats new @ cortsroyalink on Instagram

COLORKINGTATTOOS.COM

From Japanese style to surreal black and gray,
to watercolors and computer art, we have
something you will love. Prints
ranging in size from 11" x 17" to
40" x 50" will adjust the visual appeal
of any room.

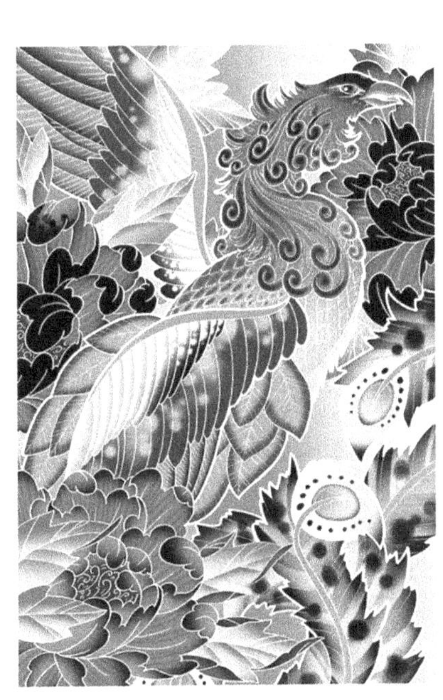

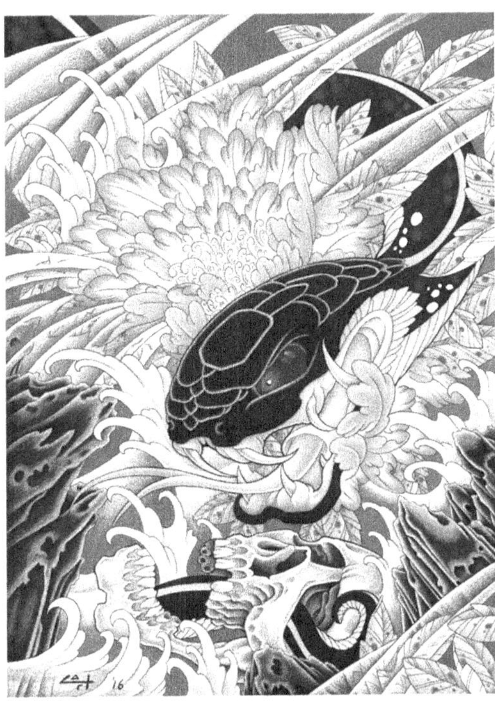

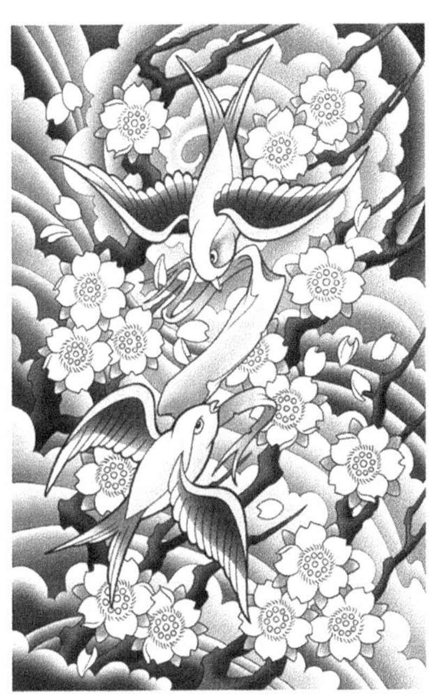

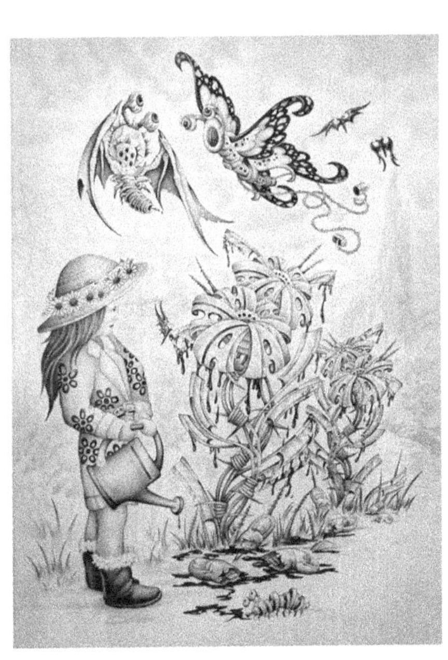

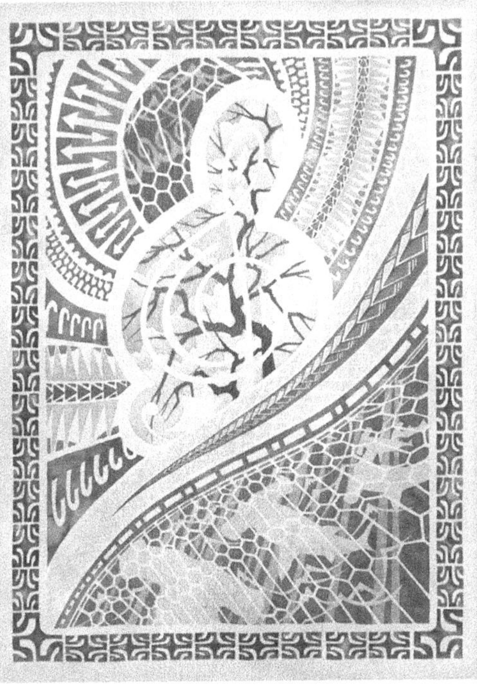

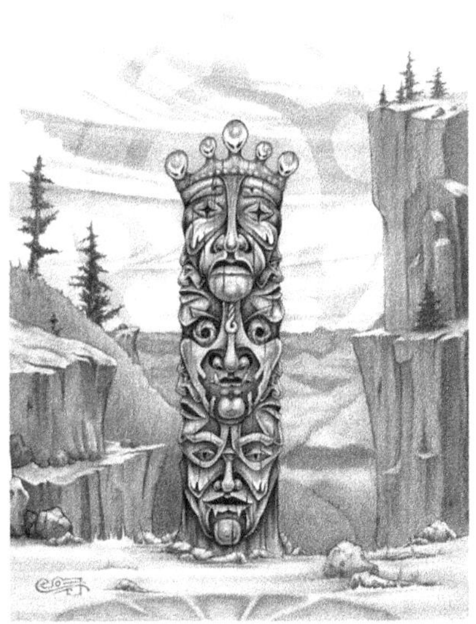